Seasons in the Garden

To: Christine

Seasons in the Garden
May all your seasons
be filled with
grace and peace

Sandra Fischer

Sandra Fischer

SEASONS IN THE GARDEN
ISBN 0996838007
ISBN 978-0-9968380-0-9

Copyright 2015 by Sandra Fischer
Interior Formatting and Cover by Penoaks Publishing,
http://penoaks.com
Edited by Jan Ackerson
Published by Evergood Books
St. Helena Island, SC
fishnet@islc.net

Unless otherwise noted, Scripture quotations are taken from the following:

Scripture taken from the ESV® Bible (The Holy Bible, English Standard Version®, copyright © 2001 by Crossway, a publishing ministry of Good News Publishers. Used by permission. All rights reserved.

Scripture taken from the Holy Bible, NEW INTERNATIONAL VERSION®, NIV® Copyright © 1973, 1978, 1984, 2011 by Biblica, Inc.® Used by permission. All rights reserved worldwide.

Scripture quotations taken from the New American Standard Bible®, Copyright © 1960, 1962, 1963, 1968, 1971, 1972, 1973, 1975, 1977, 1995 by The Lockman Foundation. Used by permission." (www.Lockman.org)

Printed by IngramSpark

To Craig
who helped create and tend
our garden of special flowers
Jamie, Sarah, and Jaren
and to our heirloom seedlings -
Olivia, Sydney, and Addie Grace

To the Dataw Island Garden Club members
who over many years helped me to appreciate
the garden where I was transplanted and
who willingly shared their
knowledge and friendship

Table of Contents

Fall

Winter

Foreword

THE FOLLOWING REFLECTIONS of seasons in life's garden grew out of a personal awareness of the constantly changing world around and within us as we travel through life's journey. Many are specific to Dataw Island, South Carolina, where my husband and I retired, and most were written particularly for the Dataw Island Garden Club.

This Low Country, as the area is called, is lush with all kinds of natural beauty. Marshes teem with plant and sea life, creating a rich aroma of pluff mud gracing the land through daily tides. Migrating birds stop to refresh themselves in their semi-annual travels. Myriad blossoms from thousands of tree and plant species appear in every season. It is here I have found a garden rich in natural beauty and filled with friends who appreciate what the Creator has given.

Life Began in a Garden

ON THE THIRD DAY OF CREATION, God planted a garden simply by speaking it into existence: "Let the land produce vegetation, seed-bearing plants and trees on the land that bear fruit with seed in it, according to their various kinds" (Genesis 1:11 NIV).

The Bible says, "it was so ... and God saw that it was good" (Genesis 1:11a-12b ESV). On the sixth day, He created the first gardener, Adam. Just as amazingly as He had created the world and all its creatures, He created man from the garden soil itself and charged him to tend it as well as to rule over all the creatures on land and sea.

So life began on earth in a garden, and the seasonal cycle instilled in Eden has continued according to the plan of the Master Gardener—Creator God. Since the beginning of time on earth, the sequence has continued. Birth, flowering, fruit-bearing, and regeneration occur in natural succession in plants, animals, and humans alike. The seeds of plants and the progeny of animals are legacies to the cycle; yet the gardener is the only creature made in the image of the Creator with a will to freely choose how to govern the earth-garden. The heart of a gardener resides within all people—the need to procreate, to nurture, and to produce. In addition, the parallels to the seasons of nature and the life of humankind are many.

Each seasonal cycle is full of all the gardener experiences in life—blessing, struggle, growth, fruit-bearing, rest—not only in our flesh but in our spirit as well. The garden is replete with lessons for all of us as the seasons pass. If we look carefully for them and glean their truths, we will experience a joyful harvest. If we are wise, we will replenish the garden by planting legacy seeds of what we've learned for our children and for those who follow us to continue the cycle.

Spring

And Spring arose on the garden fair,
Like the Spirit of Love felt everywhere;
And each flower and herb on Earth's dark breast
rose from the dreams of its wintry rest ~

Percy Bysshe Shelley

SPRING IS THE MOST NATURAL TIME to begin reflecting about seasons, because we associate birth and rebirth with spring; yet just like a baby in the womb, a great deal has been happening in field and flower before birth occurs. Seeds are germinating and while roots are stretching downward, sap is beginning to rise up tree trunks – all hidden from our eyes until a green shoot bursts forth, a blossom unfolds overnight, or the landscape is suddenly emerald instead of gold.

When I lived in Indiana, spring came in spurts, birthed in false labor pains with crocus bearing snowy coats and tulips bowing heads as if they were embarrassed about showing up too soon. Since moving to Dataw Island, South Carolina, I've noticed spring is just as reluctant to declare herself delivered, but she emerges much sooner and, because the transitory weather changes are not as pronounced, she settles in with a burst of brilliance like fireworks in July – dogwood, redbud and all shades of azalea.

Some of the spring season glimpses that follow are specific to Dataw Island and were produced as inspirations for the Dataw Island Garden Club.

Coming to My Senses

It's coming, I can feel it—
The warm breath of the wind,
Blowing soft and gentle kisses—
It's coming back again!

I heard it when a robin
Puffed out his bright red breast—
He sang the song that said "I'm back"
And woke me from my rest.

I tasted raindrops clean and new
And drank them as they fell,
Quenching thirst down deep inside,
Replenishing my well.

I smelled a hint of heady scent
Promised from a vine,
Intoxicating fragrance sweet—
Bouquet of heaven's wine.

I saw the sunlight cast its glow
Upon a brown limb's fold,
Coaxing forth a touch of green
That soon would turn to gold.

Senses dulled by Winter's sleep
Awakened with new birth,
Rejoicing at the evidence—
I, Spring, am back to earth.

… for behold, the winter is past; the rain is over and gone. The flowers appear on the earth, the time of singing has come

– The Song of Solomon 2:11-12a

Worth the Wait

Spring is coming! The proof is seen in buds peeking out from seemingly barren limbs, brown landscapes yielding their somber hues to green, and blossoms suddenly bursting alive with all the colors of the Master Painter's palette. The evidence of renewal is showing clearly and making the case—spring is coming around again.

I find it hard to imagine that only a short time ago, the same world looked rather dull and lifeless. Yet in the dark reaches of soil and branch, seeds were preparing for their seasonal debut. In a world filled with desire for instant gratification, we are usually more interested in the finished product than in the preparation. This brings back pleasant memories of my grandmother.

Grandma had an orchard that produced about every kind of fruit one could imagine. At harvest time, she would call us each Sunday morning and say, "Come out and get a pie, I have some cooling in the window."

It was so easy just to go and pick up a warm, juicy pie for our dessert. Eventually, as I learned about the process of making those pies, I gained a whole new perspective about them.

First, Grandma gathered the fruit from the orchard, peeled and pitted it, if needed, and washed it. Then, in the wee hours of Sunday morning, she would get up, stoke the kitchen stove with wood, mix and roll out the dough, pat it into the pie pans, fill them with a mixture of fruit, sugar, and flour, dot the sweetness with butter, place the top dough over all, brush each with milk or more butter, and then put the creations in the oven to bake.

The precious time she spent in making the pies was the most wonderful ingredient in the gift. Each apple, peach or raspberry pie (my favorite) was filled with love. When I considered the whole process, the pies became even more delicious in my heart.

And so it is with spring—the preparation is part of the gift. Time is the necessary element in every process of growth; learning to appreciate that makes us savor the end result all the more. Spring is worth the wait.

And let us not grow weary of doing good, for in due season we will reap,
If we do not give up

– Galatians 6:9

Horticultural Nonsense and Other Trade-offs

The "donning of the green" is at hand in the month of March. I'm not talking about celebrating St. Patrick's Day, but about greening up lawns. Have you noticed how hard people work to grow green lawns? They spend large amounts of money, time, and energy getting the proper sod or seed, applying weed-killers, fertilizer, and water—all to grow green grass. Then they do a strange thing—they cut the grass and throw it away. Sometimes they even hire others to do it for them.

They use the same logic with deciduous trees. They pamper and fertilize them so they will bear blossoms and leaves. And what do they do when they shed the leaves? They gather them up and haul them away. Later, the same people who slaved over their rakes to rid their yards of leaves buy mulch to put around trees and bushes to protect them. Where do they get the mulch? From ground-up trees!

Such illogical perspectives are observable in practices other than in horticulture. For example, some people drive thirty miles to fill up at a station selling gas for ten cents less a gallon than one near them—all to avoid being wasteful. Other people order a Diet Coke with a hot fudge sundae—to avoid being "waistful."

Mark Twain said, "Wherever you come near the human race there are layers and layers of nonsense." Yet there's something about the smell of fresh-cut grass, the sound of leaves rustling under a rake, and the taste of hot fudge. Life is full of trade-offs, whether they make sense or not. Besides, if we do enough yard work, we could order a double sundae.

Perhaps it all might make sense if we view what is lasting from an eternal perspective—to realize some of the things in which we invest our time and treasure do not make the return we really need. Laying up treasure in heaven will be more fruitful and lasting.

. . . but lay up for yourselves treasures in heaven, where neither moth nor rust destroys and where thieves do not break in and steal

– Matthew 6:20

March—the Masquerader

Here she comes, bustling into our midst with her captivating countenance, breezy and fresh—all aglow with a charming, sunny smile. How quickly winter memories melt away! But just when we relax in the warm promise of her appearing, basking in her balmy presence, thinking she has come to stay—almost as suddenly she disappears, blowing an icy kiss as she steals away.

How fickle she is—teasing us with crocus and daffodil embroidered on her clothing. She hums along with the robin's song and spins pink cotton-candy clouds on the sunset horizon just before she abruptly turns on her heel and slams the door with a huffy gust.

Every year many succumb to her subtle ambivalence, allowing themselves to believe she is Spring come early—desiring to make herself at home—only to discover the truth. It's simply March, the Masquerader, displaying her split personality, parading through in transitory fashion—bleating one day like a lamb, roaring on the next like a lion. Yet those who know her ways have learned the wisdom of patience—if March comes, she'll also leave, and an April spring cannot be far behind.

It was one of those March days when the sun shines hot and the wind blows cold; when it is summer in the light and winter in the shade

– Charles Dickens: *Great Expectations*

The Gold within the Green

March isn't just for the Irish; anyone can appreciate the earth's "wearin' o' the green." Putting on the mantle is an obvious part of spring—leaves and grasses turning into various shades of emerald, jade, lime, and olive. Most of us give only a cursory consideration to the plant life that graces the earth. We might appreciate the carpeted beauty of grass, the shade a tree provides, or the blossoms they produce, and then we leave it at that. Even diehard gardeners may not stop to reflect upon the deepest treasure replete in the plants they cultivate. Yet if we remember a basic biology lesson regarding the wonderful life-giving purpose of plants and trees, we see them in a renewed light.

They take a little sunshine, a few carbon dioxide molecules out of the air, some hydrogen atoms out of water, and then shuffle them around inside green chloroplasts in the plant cells, and *voila!* We get their products of glucose and oxygen, two necessary components to our existence.

In God's marvelous ecological economy, green plants and trees were created as our necessary counterpart—they breathe in the carbon dioxide we make and exhale the oxygen we need. Martin Luther said, "In the true nature of things . . . every green tree is far more glorious than if it were made of gold and silver."

If I see some people hugging trees or watering even weeds, I know they appreciate how precious our green earth is.

The trees of the LORD are watered abundantly, the cedars of Lebanon that He planted

– Psalm 104:16

Spring Pruning—Inside and Out

Getting ready for spring always meant pruning at our house. My father, the gardener, would wield his shears on overgrown shrubs and trees. He understood the process of renewal by pruning dead wood and allowing the plants' support systems to send vital energy and nutrients to a smaller area, thus encouraging more vigorous growth. The plants gained a more attractive appearance, and their flower and fruit production increased.

My mother, the indoor pruner, applied the same principle to every drawer and closet in our house. We had to prune whatever it was we weren't using or wearing and find a new home for it. Clothes, toys, books, and knick-knacks soon made their way to other families or charities.

Not only did our house improve in appearance, but with less stuff to manage, our spirits were renewed by a sense of order and peace.

Studies have shown that the pruning principle has a positive effect on humans as well as on plants. If we submit to God's pruning, He will help us rid our lives of excess, whether material things, negative attitudes, or destructive habits. We will become less stressed and less depressed, healthier and more energetic in body and spirit.

Each time we sharpen our pruning shears, we need to think "inside the box." We need to consider carefully what needs to be trimmed or removed from within ourselves to help us mature.

I am the true vine, and my Father is the vinedresser. Every branch in me that does not bear fruit he takes away, and every branch that does bear fruit he prunes, that it may bear more fruit

– John 15:1-2

Planting Seeds

Spring is seed planting time, yet most of us impatient gardeners bypass that process by buying plants all ready for bedding. However, if we dig deeper in our consideration of seed planting, we will find that all of us, whether gardeners or not, are sowing seeds. These seeds, which germinate in our minds, can root and burst forth in speech and action. Some, like seeds of kindness, will enjoy a perpetual harvest. Others become weeds, choking out the growth of the hardiest, most desirable plants. Most of us desire to plant only those seeds that will beautify our garden spaces.

No one deliberately says, "I guess I'll sow some criticism by my neighbor's fence today, or fill this window box with bitter complaining, so I can enjoy it when I look out." Hardly.

Seeds of discontent are usually blown about with a sudden breath of carelessness. When we realize what could be the fruit of our rashness, we pray for a crop failure. A wise gardener considers the principles of sowing and reaping before plowing ahead. He would agree to the insight of Ralph Waldo Emerson: "Sow a thought, reap an action; sow an action, reap a habit; sow a habit, reap an attitude; sow an attitude, reap a destiny."

Every day is seed planting time—we just need to choose those seeds that will fill the gardens of our lives with sheaves of joy.

Do not be deceived: God is not mocked, for whatever one sows, that will he also reap

– Galatians 6:7

Co-op Gardening

I did my part—
Sketched a plot
Amended the soil
Dug a trough

Embedded the seeds
Pre-emerged
Watered and fed
Mulched in hope

Now it's up to
Heaven's part
To provide what
I cannot—

Rays of sun
Periods of shade
Showers of rain
For flowers of blessing

So neither he who plants nor he who waters is anything but only God gives the growth

– 1 Corinthians 3:7

Spring's Eternal Cheerfulness

Crocuses are said to represent cheerfulness—a fitting name for the first heralds of spring, particularly after a long, cold winter. Little did the fifteenth-century monks in Husum, Germany realize how much cheerfulness they were planting when they hoped to raise orange crocuses for the saffron produced by the flowers. They planted the wrong strain, however, and abandoned the endeavor. But their mistake is enjoyed today by spring visitors to Purple Park near Husum, where the glorious sight of over four million purple crocuses greets them in colorful array.

Like the monks in Husum, we plant seeds in our relationships of what we hope will produce good fruit. We speak words, sometimes carelessly, and expect them to grow. We don't see immediate results, so we grow weary and think nothing is happening—yet God, in His infinite wisdom, patience, and providence nourishes those seeds into a springtime of beauty beyond our limited imaginations. Sometimes relationships develop into something more beautiful than we had expected, and may yield blessings beyond our dreams.

Alexander Pope wrote, "Hope springs eternal." We could say that Spring gives us eternal hope, especially when we plant seeds of cheerfulness and leave the results to God.

Words are seeds – they land in our hearts and not the ground. Be careful what you plant and careful what you say. You might have to eat what you planted one day

– Ritu Ghatourey

A Garden of IPO's

(Investment Planting Of Seeds)

When we plant seeds, we're investing in tiny objects of promise—looking forward to a future of flowering returns. We do our part—providing good soil, fertilizer, and tender care. We shelter them from weeds, blight, and disease by protecting them, and we pray for a ratio of sun and rain that will yield a garden of dividends.

Much of what seeds become is a result of what gardeners believe about them. So it is with people. Successful people tell us that someone influenced them, nourished them, encouraged and supported them. Someone believed in them. Consider this note attached to an ivy plant given to a caring teacher by her students: "Because of the seeds you planted in us, we will one day grow into beautiful plants like this one . . . thank you for investing time in our lives."

It's true. All the flowers of all the tomorrows are in the seeds of today. They are the seeds of hope that produce flowers of joy. To become a successful Seed Investment Planter, we need to take stock in those around us who need attention. We must bond with those who show interest in growing. The people in whom we invest will make long-term gains, and the world will become richer for it. To have such a successful garden, we need to get sowing.

The point is this: whoever sows sparingly will also reap sparingly, and whoever sows bountifully will also reap bountifully

– 2 Corinthians 9:6

Seeds and Fruit

I read a fable once about a man browsing in a garden store, when he made the shocking discovery that God was behind the sales counter in the seed section. So the man walked over and asked, "What are you selling?"

God answered, "What does your heart desire?"

"I want happiness, peace of mind, and freedom from fear … for me and for the whole world."

God smiled and said, "I don't sell fruit here, only seeds."

The importance of sowing the right kind of seeds has been noted in scripture—"Whatever one sows, that he will also reap" (Galatians 6:7b). Sowing our own seeds is significant as well. We can't expect to experience the fruit of God's blessings if we don't recognize that we share an important part in planting the garden. It's never the wrong season to be planting seeds of new actions and responses in life, and in due time we will enjoy the increase.

> We're always sowing seeds in life
> By everything we do and say,
> So let's make sure the fruit we reap
> Comes from the good we do each day ~
> Hess

With every deed you're sowing a seed, though the harvest you may not see

– Ella Wheeler Wilcox

Consider the Lilies

One of my world-travelled friends told me she had visited the most beautiful structure in the world—the Taj Mahal in India. Intricately inlaid with mosaic marble, this famous mausoleum took over twenty years to construct, and it stands as a testimony to humanity's ability to create iconic architecture. Recently, while delivering some event flyers to a local neighborhood, I came upon a garden of stunning beauty, filled with at least a dozen amaryllis standing tall and trumpeting spring without a sound. Vibrant with pink and red, their striped petals openly displayed unrivaled natural splendor to anyone blessed to feast eyes upon them.

I thought about the Taj Mahal and how its glory has attracted people for nearly 400 years, and then I considered the amaryllis. Both creations represent magnificence. A verse from the Gospel of Luke makes a similar comparison: *Consider the lilies, how they grow. They neither toil nor spin. Yet I tell you even Solomon in all his glory was not arrayed like one of these"* (Luke 12:27 ESV).

Indeed, people have created some magnificent structures worthy of admiration. Some, like the Taj Mahal, still exist, but who cannot marvel each spring at the radiance of one single flower inherently arrayed? Besides—the Taj Mahal is 7,000 miles away, while lilies grace a garden just outside my back door.

Human subtlety...will never devise an invention more beautiful, more simple or more direct than does nature, because in her inventions nothing is lacking, and nothing is superfluous

– Leonardo Da Vinci

How to Spell "Dataw Spring"

Daffodils like trumpets
Azaleas all aflame
Tulips lining walkways
Amaryllis in the rain
Wax begonia cushions
Snapdragons rearing heads
Petunias and pansies and
Roses, oh, so red!
Iris splendor budding
New Guineas "impatiening"
Geranium in full splendor
It's really **DATAW SPRING!**

Faithfulness springs up from the ground,
and righteousness looks down from the sky

– Psalm 85:11 ESV

Remembering Springtime in Indiana

When I reflect on springtime in Indiana, I remember morel mushrooms. Hunting them and enjoying them in various culinary forms was a long-standing tradition in my family. My mother was the foremost morel aficionado, but one spring Mother couldn't go mushroom hunting. After having surgery, she was recuperating at home. No scurrying off to the Hoosier woodlands to hunt the rare cone-shaped mushrooms, which have a short growing season. For Mother that was a real hardship; mushrooming was her gift.

Every year we kids would trail along, fanning out in different directions, searching in proven breeding grounds—patches of mayapple, rotting stumps, and fallen elm. But it was always Mother who called out suddenly, "Come see what I've found!" And in an unpromising pile of decaying leaves, half-hidden, would be precious honeycomb morel spikes peeking out.

I didn't understand all the fuss. "Why can't we just plant them in our garden and save the trouble of hunting them?"

Mother smiled, explaining that these mushrooms were special, sent by God to delight us. "He chooses where they grow."

That spring, Mother longed to go mushrooming, but instead, she puttered listlessly in the garden. One day, while she was watering the tulips, I heard her cry, "Come see what I've found!"

There among the flowers I spotted something familiar—a morel! Soon we spied several, growing where they never had grown before—and never have since. Mother couldn't go to the mushrooms, so God sent them to her. I often think of how God blessed Mother with the desires of her heart that day. He delights in giving us our desires when we delight in Him.

Delight yourself in the Lord, and He will give you the desires of your hear

– Psalm 37:4

Seasonal Transitions

Spring was on the calendar, but no one told the clouds
Defiant as they gathered thick and spat a bitter rain
A robin fluttered in the yard bringing hope anew
Then icy winds blew it away with coated frosty breath
Donning sweaters once again, we yearned for summer past
Forgetting sweat's revulsion and how we longed for coolness
Transitions seem so endless—it's the other thing we want
Clouds on sweltering dog days, sun when winter overstays
And just as we begin to yield our wants and take what is
Forsaking discontented time with gritted teeth to bear it
Spring finally waltzes in on tempered sunny breezes
Forcing us to change perspectives on seasonal transitions
Yes, in the meantime solace comes with wisdom's way—
To everything there is a season and this, too, shall pass

He changes times and seasons; he removes kings and sets up kings; he gives wisdom to the wise and knowledge to those who have understanding

– Daniel 2:21

Nothing to Sneeze At

"Earth's crammed with heaven and every common bush afire with God." How appropriate are these lines by Elizabeth Barrett Browning to describe the Dataw Island landscape in spring! Amazing azaleas demand the attention their gloriously colored blossoms deserve, while dogwood, redwood, and flowering fruit trees beg us to appreciate them as well.

People who appreciate this amazing natural display gain an important bonus. Recent studies on health indicate that people who take a moment to consider their surroundings each day and appreciate the beauty therein are much happier and healthier than those who don't.

Of course, some pollen allergy sufferers may disagree with what springtime blossoming can create for them. They are thinking, "Whoever said *take time to smell the roses* didn't have allergies!" Yet they probably know, too, that without pollination all the earth's ecosystems and the human race itself would not survive. So for these people, welcoming the unfolding of spring is a mixed blessing. By all accounts, particularly those made by our senses, spring is unrivaled in its evidence of God's marvelous creation, its promise of renewal, and its provision of regeneration. And that's nothing to sneeze at.

I love spring anywhere, but if I could choose I would always greet it in a garden

– Ruth Stout

Dataw Island's Spring Fashion Show

The curtain's up at Dataw
On a virtual fashion show
Beauties on the runway
Strutting, all aglow

Camellia's gowned in pink and red
With streaks on velvet white
Framed in leaves of deep dark green—
A truly breathless sight.

Azalea wears a large hoop skirt
That rustles in the breeze,
Shades of scarlet feathers
Gathered round her knees.

Redbud, Dogwood, Cherry
Have blossoms in their hair,
Limbs flowing so gracefully
Like angel-wings on air.

*Now every field is clothed with grass
and every tree with leaves;
now the woods put forth their blossoms
and the year assumes its gay attire*

Amaryllis, Jasmine
Lily, Iris, Rose
Peek out behind the curtain
While practicing a pose.

– Virgil

The Master of Design looks down,
A smile upon His face—
Pleased to see His fashions
Shown with style and grace.

What gorgeous frocks and models -
Nothing could be "finah"
Than applauding yet another spring
In Dataw, South Carolina.

Early Riser

Was it overwhelming warmth
Seeping through Winter's dark cover
Stirring her awake?
Or sun rays peeking through cloud curtains?
Perhaps a balmy zephyr called—*Arise*
Rousing her to stretch leggy roots,
Thrust leafy arms upward
And bound from her bed of Spring dreams.

Bursting forth, shedding
Earth's blanket, she stands—
Heralding the day,
Clad in brilliant attire,
Blossoming forth in unrivaled beauty,
Petaled face aglow with dreams come true.
A welcome surprise, this early riser's *Hello!*
An April flower come to March morning.

The flowers appear on the earth, the time of singing has come, and the voice of the turtledove is heard in our land

– Song of Solomon 2:12

Musings of a South Carolina Transplant

Spring is typically a time to do transplanting. I read an article outlining some key considerations about the process, and it occurred to me it offered some parallels to my life. After having lived in Indiana in the same home for over 35 years, my husband and I retired to Dataw Island, South Carolina. We took up residence in a community of other retirees from various other states, and it dawned on me—we were all *transplants*. Some of the key considerations in the article applied to us:

Transplanting can cause stress; plants can become unattractive. Leaving our home after so many years and moving to an area where we knew few people made me homesick and grumpy, causing some unpleasant moments in our new home.

Some plants need root pruning before moving. Pulling up our roots meant saying goodbye to family, friends and business associates, ties that would be stretched by the miles put between us.

New site conditions, water, and mulch are important. Despite the stress of moving, we found the site conditions to be excellent. The semi-tropical landscape gave us a broad spectrum of seasonal flora, from deciduous trees to palm and pine. The milder winter (no snow on the pine branches) kept our gardens and our hearts warm enough for buds to emerge and new flowering to grow as we adapted to the coastal environment. Our many new friends were like "water and mulch" to us helping us to settle in and establish our roots.

Seasons can affect transplants. Our new season in life affected us by encouraging us to grow and adapt to new possibilities as we found new ways to enjoy life and appreciate a different garden.

Plants already in decline may likely succumb to transplantation stress. While we were in our advancing years when we moved here, we adapted to the soil and have not succumbed. Rather, we are blessed, and we are blooming where we were "trans"planted.

The righteous will flourish like a palm tree, They will grow like a cedar of Lebanon, Planted in the house of the LORD.

— Psalm 90: 12

April Symphony

Rhythmic raindrops
On rooftop resound
Piccolo chirps from
Crickets by the pond

Wind rustling leaves
Brush-sticks on snare
Double bass thunder
Rattling the air

Caw-caw of crow
Trumpets in the trees
Syncopated patters
Drip from hanging eaves

Hautboy—the oboe
In duck calls abound
Soft muted horn
Pigeon on the ground

Brown wren trilling
Flautist on the wing
Bumblebees buzzing
Bow on viol string

What an orchestration
Set in nature's key
Joyful sounds of spring—
An April symphony

The earth has music for those who listen

– George Santayana

Ever-present Gold Minding

Each spring I ponder Robert Frost's poem "Nothing Gold Can Stay":

> Nature's first green is gold
> Her hardest hue to hold
> Her early leaf's a flower
> But only so an hour
> Then leaf subsides to leaf
> So Eden sank to grief
> And dawn goes down to day
> Nothing gold can stay.

Such profound reflection on life's passing might seem pessimistic at first glance, yet the reality of constant change can cause us to embrace the moment, cherish the present and celebrate each season with gratitude. Consider the daylily—its blossoms last only a day. Clothed in exquisite beauty, each petal makes a quick, glorious debut, and just as suddenly exits the stage, its one-time performance completed. We can either choose to enjoy the brief blessing it brings or bemoan its quick demise. If we receive the blessing, we realize the faithfulness of the One who made the lily. Contained within the flower is a new blossom of gold, ready to appear the very next day, and the next.

Yes, blossoms fade, gold tarnishes, life passes. But each moment, each day, each season is replete with its own treasures ready to be mined and minded with joy and appreciation as they come, and go, and come again.

So teach us to number our days that we may get a heart of wisdom

– Psalm 90:12

April Showers Bring May...

There it was
One small raindrop
Kissing my forehead
Another caught on my
Outstretched tongue

Then one upon another
Drenched me fresh
Magnified by the
Sudden flash of spotlight
On sky and cloud and leaf

Followed by the roar
Of Heaven's applause
For April's performance
And the curtain rising
On blossoming merry May

Ask rain from the LORD in the season of the spring rain, from the LORD who makes the storm clouds, and he will give them showers of rain, to everyone the vegetation in the field

– Zechariah 10:1

Our Treasure Island

"Acres of Diamonds" is a story that has been told by Temple University founder Russell Conwell over five thousand times. It is the true story of a successful landowner in India who sells his land to search the world for diamonds. Years later, he dies penniless, never having found diamonds. Back home, the man who purchased the land discovers a huge field of diamonds right on the land the man sold him.

So often we are like the original landowner—looking for riches everywhere else, only to discover they exist in our own backyards. What treasure might we find on our own island? One need only take a stroll during the month of May to see a wealth of beauty in our gardens and common grounds. Such jewels as jasmine adorn arches, trees, and message posts. Panning the landscape, one can strike a claim on both goldenrod and marigold. A gerbera ruby-red daisy stands tall in a border display, and pearlwort lines a walkway. Hummingbirds hover over the petals of coral-bells near a birdbath and a potted silver jade succulent graces a patio table. It's possible to discover an amethyst or sapphire plant blooming nearby and some diamond frost plants as well, although we need sight only one, not an acre, to illustrate the wealth we have underfoot.

Some will say they'd rather have the real diamonds and gold, but the measure of true wealth is contentment. As a wise man noted, "He is richest who is content with the least, for contentment is the wealth of nature." That man was Socrates—and if he could see the rich splendor of Dataw Island in the month of May, he might call it a truly "*a-May-zing Treasure Island!*"

Whoever loves and understands a garden will find contentment within

– Chinese proverb

Just Singin' For the Rain

Springtime means spring rains, but sometimes they disrupt our parades. Gardening, golf and beachcombing plans are always subject to the whims of weather. Bemoaning the interruption to our good pleasures, we complain, "Every time I plan to . . .it *has* to rain." Such reflections are short-sighted, clouded over by the fact that it really does *have* to rain. Without it we would have no gardens, golf courses, or beaches at all, nor would we be around to enjoy them. Rain is a precious commodity, providing one of the basic elements of life we many times take for granted: water.

Consider the wonder of water. Effectively, all living things on earth are composed mostly of water, depend on it, or live in it. Adult humans are composed of 60-65 percent water, and if we're thinking some people just have it on their brains—we're partly right. The fact is, all human brains are 75 percent water. Water is necessary to the physiology of all life. It serves as a natural air conditioning system for regulating the temperature of our bodies and is a thermostat for the earth itself.

Consider the beauty of water. It reveals itself in clouds shaped into glorious patterns, in frost laced upon a window pane, in dew shimmering on flower blossoms, in tides mirroring marshes, and in rainbows infused with glorious color. Whether as mist or fog, frost or snowflake, dewdrop or raindrop, water is a wonderful blessing to all of us in God's marvelous creation.

So when April showers threaten to ruin your sunny day plans, just grab your umbrella, head outside, and start "Singin' *for* the Rain"!

For as the rain and snow come down from heaven and do not return there but water the earth making it bring forth and sprout, giving seed to the sower and bread to the eater

– Isaiah 55:10

Tribute to Southern Spring

Here among pine and palm
Where white ibis dip their toes
In reedy tidal marsh

And birdsong echoes
Wake us in insistent prelude
To the dawning of the day

And fragrant blossoms
Borne on gentle breeze
Invite butterfly and bee to feast

And trees shed winter coats
Wrinkled leaf, straw, and cone
Revealing green and gold

And all creation sings God's praises
His eternal power, divine nature
Clearly seen in flower, field, and sky

And we—last of creatures made—
Marvel at unfolding life
God-awesome mystery of it all

And put our pen to paper,
Brush to canvas, sound to score
Scarce keeping any of its wonder

Here among magnolia and myrtle
Where earth ever turns its face to sun,
Beaming at this southern Spring!

O Lord, how manifold are your works! In wisdom have you made
them all; the earth is full of your creatures

— *Psalm 104:24*

Summer

In summer, the song sings itself

William Carlos Williams

SUMMERTIME IS THE SEASON of maturation. Flowers are in full bloom on both stem and vine, showing forth myriad colors and blossoms. Here in the Low Country, azalea, lily, rose, magnolia, and hydrangea perennially command our attention as they return to the landscape in sassy blossoming. Grass and marsh have greened up, while palm and pine shed their spent fronds and straw. Cloudbursts come and go, bringing moisture to the thirsty ground, cooling the land and releasing nitrates that fertilize the soil.

The earth is alive with nature's summer serenade—cardinal song at dawn, cricket and frog at dusk, and the buzz of bee and hummingbird at day between. The long song of cicada rise and fall—a fitting representation of the season. Temperatures, tides, and thunderstorms come with a crescendo, then diminish and fade.

Our lives parallel the season, too. We pass from the springtime of youth into a form of adulthood—full of cocky confidence as we leave our awkward, budding adolescence and flower into the prime of life. We are vibrant and alive, full of expectation and drive. We flower with an unreasoned assurance that we will live forever. In the subsoil of our hearts, however, we begin to have a sense of the reality of time's passing—and thus will the season pass, also.

Memorial Flowers and Food for Thought

Memorial Day has long been associated with the beginning of summer. Placing and planting flowers at gravesites is a prevalent practice in our country. However, some Americans bring other cultural traditions as memorials.

An American of Chinese origin placed a bowl of rice at a gravesite, which is a common practice for those of his ethnic background. He was observed by someone putting flowers on a nearby burial site as a tribute.

"When is your friend going to arise and eat that food?" the observer asked with a smile.

Without hesitation, the first man replied with a similar smile, "When yours comes up to smell his flowers."

Why do we use flowers as memorials?

Using flowers at funerals came into practice in America as late as the 19th century for the purpose their masking fragrance provided before a delayed burial could take place. Later, even after embalming became prevalent, the custom continued, prompting an anonymous writer to pen this perspective about floral memorials:

I would rather have one little rose
From the garden of a friend,
Than to have the choicest flowers
When my stay on earth must end.

I would rather have one pleasant word
In kindness said to me,
Than flattery when my heart is still
And life has ceased to be.

I would rather have a loving smile
From friends I know are true,
Than tears shed 'round my casket,
When the world I bid adieu.

Blossoms bring to me today
Whether pink or white or red;
I'd rather have one blossom now,
Than a truckload when I'm dead.

Flowers add beauty to any occasion, and when given at funerals or as memorials, they are a reminder of how fleeting life is. Giving flowers anytime can be a blessing, but giving and receiving the love they represent is of the essence while we're living.

All flesh is like grass and all its glory like the flower of grass. The grass withers, and the flower falls

— 1 Peter 1:24

Cultivating a Friendship Garden

Cultivating a garden can be likened to how we develop friendships. Some people start by planting little seeds: a smile, a kind word, a compliment, a caring gesture, a sharing of commonalities, a helping hand, or a listening ear. Soon these small gestures of friendship sprout into a wide variety of flowers and plants. Some spring up quickly, while others take time to root and bloom.

As wise gardeners know, plants grow and thrive if they are nurtured properly with care and love. This is also true of friendships—just as flowers need sunlight, water, air, and soil to blossom, so friendships need warmth, refreshment, space, and encouragement to develop. How then do we cultivate relationships we want to blossom?

We pay attention. We make ourselves available. We learn as much as possible about each individual's needs. We take note of what pleases and what doesn't. Some people like the sunshine given by the warmth of our presence; others need to be frequently watered with kind and encouraging words. Some need the refreshing air of a quiet listening ear, and all need enriched soil for support. The healthiest gardens—and the healthiest friendships—are kept free of weeds. Slights, jealousy, negativity, and indifference are pulled up quickly so grudges won't become a blight.

With constant, loving attention, plants and friendships become well-rooted, able to weather arid periods, hard frosts, and storms. The result is that we can experience the perennial blessings and joy both kinds of flourishing gardens bring all year long.

Two are better than one, because they have a good reward for their toil. For if they fall, one will lift up his fellow. But woe to him who is alone when he falls and has not another to lift him up

– Ecclesiastes 4:9-10

Saving for Those Rainy Days

Sometimes seasons bring a series of rainy days when it seems as if clouds have completely blotted out the sun. Many times, this is a reflection of the challenging days in which we live. How do people deal with storms, both on earth's landscapes and in their personal lives? Some philosophize with Longfellow, who said, "Into each life some rain must fall," others curse the downpours for spoiling their plans, while gardeners welcome them as necessary for strengthening seedlings and encouraging growth. "No rain, no gain," they might say.

I knew a lady who kept a sunshine box for stormy gales. In it were small tokens representing the happiest days of her life. A pressed flower from her wedding day, a sand dollar from a shelling expedition, and a dog-eared postcard from a Scottish pen pal—all part of her collection, saved for rainy days.

When storms showered outside or when squalls of worries clouded her mind, she would open the box and let the sunbeams of happy memories brighten her heart. "I can't choose the weather," she'd say, "but I can choose my attitude." I am reminded of Sara Teasdale's poem, "The Coin."

Into my heart's treasury
I slipped a coin
That time cannot take
Nor a thief purloin, —
Oh better than the minting
Of a gold-crowned king
Is the safe-kept memory
Of a lovely thing.

Everyone needs a sunshine box, filled with items saved to spend on rainy days.

. . .whatever is true, whatever is honorable, whatever is just, whatever is pure, whatever is lovely, whatever is commendable, if there is any excellence, if there is anything worthy of praise, think about these things.

– Philippians 4:8

Father's Day in the Garden

Spending time with my father meant spending time in the garden. It was his favorite place from spring to fall. I can see him now in his denim overalls, one hand on top of the hoe, the other swiping a red neckerchief across his sweaty, freckled brow.

"Gonna be a good crop this year," he'd say as he checked for potato bugs and inspected for corn borers. "Got to watch out for those nasty pests that can ruin your crop. Same as life; gotta keep sin-bugs away, or they'll ruin you."

Being in the garden with Dad was like attending school; he never missed an opportunity to teach life lessons sprouting at every turn. From the sowing and reaping principle to learning about patience and hard work, Dad turned my mind over to wise considerations as carefully as he did the soil.

"You can't be in a hurry for something good to grow," he'd say. "Can't just plant it and leave it—you gotta do some tending if you want success. Weeding is work, but if you stick with it and pull them out before they take root, your garden will produce good things."

I never became the gardener my father was, at least in growing potatoes and corn. I have a better legacy: a gardener's heart for perpetuating fruit-bearing by cultivating seeds of wisdom in the minds of my children and grandchildren. Thanks, Dad.

Carve your name on hearts, not tombstones. A legacy is etched into the minds of others and the stories they share about you

– Shannon L. Alder

A Honey of a Creature

Ogden Nash wrote: God in his wisdom made the fly
And then forgot to tell us why.

He might have included mosquitoes and no-see-ums, too, but there is one six-legged creature God made that is a phenomenal blessing—the honeybee.

September is designated as "National Honey Month," so it's a fitting time to recognize the makers of the world's original sweetener. If it weren't for honeybees, our food supply would be inadequate. According to Archie Biering, Bee City, South Carolina beekeeper extraordinaire, thirty percent of all our food depends upon bee pollination. The trees we see blossoming and the flowers that grace our gardens would be few and far between without these busy fellows. I should say busy *gals*, actually, because worker bees are all female. The male drones exist for one reason, and after that little encounter with the queen bee, they drop dead.

In addition to pollination, these industrious insects provide products that we use daily: not only honey, but royal jelly in lotions and cosmetics; beeswax in candles, ointments and pill coatings; and propolis, a kind of glue substance used for medical purposes. Granular bee pollen is good for treating allergies and providing energy. Scientists have revealed that honey has powerful antibacterial properties on at least sixty species of bacteria. Unlike antibiotics, which are often useless against certain types of bacteria, honey is non-toxic and has strong effects.

Perhaps we can see what all the buzz is about when we consider this honey of a creature. It inspired me to write this couplet to counterbalance the likes of Nash:

I marvel at you, honey bee—
How good of God to think of thee.

Bees work for man and yet they never bruise their Master's flower, but leave it having done as fair as ever and as fit to use; so both the flower doth stay and the honey run

– George Herbert

Dataw Island Garden Glee Club

(To the tune of "Carolina in the Mornin'")

Nothin could be harder than to be a Dataw gardener if you're all alone.
Diggin' and a hoein' thinkin' nothin' will be growin' if you're all alone.
Learning how to compost, where to plant what and when
Needs the help of those who know 'cause they've already been…there

Nothin' could be better than to learn to work together and not all alone
Using others' knowledge so we needn't go to college all on our own.
If I had some seeds to plant for only a day
I'd make a wish and here's what I'd say
Nothin' could be finer than some gardeners harmonizin' 'stead of gard'ning alone.

In gardening and in music, some people are well equipped to do solos, but a Garden Club is like a large chorus of people sharing their unique knowledge to benefit all and to create a harmonious landscape in the community.

For example, in our Garden Club we have "Seedy" people who are good at knowing all about seeds: when to plant what where. We have "Feedy" people who know everything about fertilizer and mulch. The "Weedy" people, experienced in hoeing and pulling, know every weed in the garden and how to manage each of them. Adding to the chorus are the "Deedy" people who share their time and talents by providing designs for local events. Finally, we have a few "Needy" people—truly green novice gardeners eager to learn from the experienced voices in the club.

Each gardener has a gift to share, and harmony comes when we pool our gifts and share together. By learning from each other and working in accord, we become better gardeners: Succeedy" people who reap from what we sow and share. No wonder a harmonious Garden Club is full of glee.

Harmony makes small things grow

– Sallust

"No-seeums" — Complements of God

My idea of the best beach vacation is one when it doesn't rain, and when sand and surf sparkle under clear, blue skies. My idea of the best garden is one that flourishes with plants I want in it and is free of those I don't. My idea of a perfect day on Dataw Island is one completely free of pesky bugs, especially "no-see-ums," small midges that are prevalent in this area in the summer.

Fortunately, life is not based on my ideas. I say *fortunately*, after contemplating how life is full of tradeoffs—complements that provide a balance and harmony we may never fully understand, much less appreciate.

For example: no rain—no rainbows, no weeds—no mulch, no bugs—no birds, and the list goes on. The same granule of sand that irritates an eye is the one that stimulates the oyster to make a pearl. The same bee whose sting causes pain is the one that makes the honey. The same heat and pressure that cause us to sweat is what, when compressed beneath the earth, turns a lump of coal into a diamond.

So when I begin to think the world was created just for my comfort, ease, and good pleasure, and I am bugged by the least little annoyance, such as inclement weather or "no-see-ums," I am reminded that the Creator has a plan and purpose for everything He created. The delicate balance of the universe is so intricate, and the parameters so finely tuned, even the smallest deviation would wreak havoc. All the more reason to trust God's wisdom.

Yet as I rub the welt on my arm, compliments of a "no-see-um," I still wonder about His plan to have me as a tiny midge's lunch in the food chain of life.

A single swallow, it is said, devours ten millions of insects every year. The supplying of these insects I take to be an instance of the Creator's bounty in providing for the lives of His creatures

– Attributed to Henry Ward Beecher

One Day to Blossom

One of the most beautiful blossoms that graces summer gardens is the hibiscus, a daylily. Its blossoms are some of the most dramatic of any flowering plant. Some can be as large as luncheon plates, and their bright hues of salmon and yellow are dramatic standouts against their green foliage. Each day, trumpet-shaped flowers appear, announcing their arrival with a burst of glory as they spread their petals. By evening, they fold up like an umbrella that has served its purpose. Their beauty spent, they shrivel and drop off the plant, having given all in one short, single day.

As I consider that blossom's brief life, I am reminded of the psalmist, who says: "As for man, his days are like grass, he flourishes like the flower of the field; the wind blows over it and it is gone, and its place remembers it no more" (Psalm 103:15-16).

What a great reminder to not count moments, but to make the moments count. Our days are short, and each one should be treasured as an opportunity to blossom in our own little corner of life's garden.

. . . yet you do not know what tomorrow will bring. What is your life? For you are a mist that appears for a little time and then vanishes

– James 4:14

Seeds and Stitches—Connecting the Past to the Present

What do gardens and quilting have in common? Both can include heirlooms—seeds or stitches—passed down through the years. Just as heirloom quilters touch the past and the future, so do gardeners who preserve seeds and cuttings handed down to them. For example, peonies my father grew in our Indiana family garden in the 1930s came from my grandmother's stock. Their showy blossoms continue to thrive from those same plantings as they grace my sister's yard today, fifty miles from the original plot.

Just as an heirloom quilt has a story stitched within its folds to give comfort and peace, so also many gardens have heirloom plants with memories sown within the soil. Both are legacies of people and places who entrusted them to those to whom they've been bequeathed, to blanket legacy garden beds or to cover the earth. Some Amish gardeners in Indiana have transposed quilting patterns into flower gardens and have a summer tour for those who want to view their creative designs. Their designs demonstrate the connection between seeds and stitches in binding color and form into a ground cover quilt.

Of course, it's true that many of the quilts and gardens created today are not made with patches or seeds from the past. Nevertheless, they color our lives with the beauty they bring and they may be sewing or sowing new legacies into the fabric of our lives.

The things you do for yourself are gone when you are gone, but the things you do for others remain your legacy

– Kalu Kalu

Stormy Weather

Summer weather fluctuations affect the attitude of some people. On those humid, possibly stormy days, they lament, "What a lousy day!" Actually, the day is never "lousy." The sun is still shining above the clouds, and beneath the ground, roots are stretching deeper into the earth while flowers and plants continue to grow and flourish.

In fact, the plant life we enjoy needs respite from the sun and heat to grow properly. We do, too. We need time to think, rest, pray, and refresh ourselves. Regardless of what the weather brings, and regardless of our circumstances, life continues. How we view it makes the difference. Henry Ward Beecher said, "God asks no man whether he will accept life. That is not the choice. You must take it. The only question is how."

The weather is never the problem; attitude is. And attitude is a decision we make on a moment-by-moment basis. William James said it well: "There is the negative side and the positive side and at every moment I decide." So the next time the weather is not to our liking, we need to check our *whether* report. We can decide whether or not to let the weather determine our attitude. If we choose well, neither our attitude nor the weather will be lousy.

The greater part of our happiness or misery depends upon our dispositions, and not upon our circumstances

– Martha Washington

Blindsided

Fingers poised on keys, I wait
And hope and pray—beg, actually, for
Phrases brilliantly fused to flow
From mind and digitally march
In perfect symmetry upon the page

Nothing comes. The mind is numb.
No inspirations tucked between the
Minutes of my mundane day,
Waiting for my hands to ply them
Loose and sculpt them into form.

Earlier, a cardinal woke me with his song,
Trilling forth his daybreak greeting – *Ta Da*!
Now, a chorus of wren and chickadee
Joins in, as if the day needs nothing more
Except to sing and flit about in feathered glee.

I stumble out of bed and make the coffee
Extra strong to jump-start my right brain
Into creative motion. From the open window
The sweet smell of gardenia comes -
Floating toward me on fresh-morn zephyr.

I see bees hovering in leaves of holly tree,
Buzzing in profuse pollinating pleasure.
Suddenly, two Sulphurs dance by – fluttering
Their golden-winged happiness, landing
Touch-and-go on petals sparkling with dew.

I trudge reluctantly to the computer,
Hoping for an e-mail to magically unlock
The vestiges of a muse imprisoned
In the ho-hum cells of my blocked brain.
I find two forwards and fifteen spam.

One forward is filled with breathtaking
Photographs – ice-covered canyons and
Desert sand sculptures shaped by God,
Ribbons of northern lights aglow -
Awash with undulating waves of color.

The other forward – an ad for struggling
Writers: "How to Remove the Blinds from
The Inspiration Windows of Your Mind
In Five Easy Steps – Guaranteed."
Desperate – I click the banner to sign up.

Inspiration and blessings abound if we would open the eyes of our heart to see

– Sandra Fischer

Those Pesky Besetting Weeds

It's no surprise when weeds pop up in a garden that's been tilled and fertilized; they love to grow in conditions we intend only for chosen plants and flowers. But when they suddenly appear on an asphalt driveway with no obvious cracks or on a paver patio grouted with thick cement, we wonder at their resolve and tenacity. How in the world did those pesky, relentless plants find just the right spot to shoulder their way up and out from the thickest kind of ground cover?

Weeds crop up in our daily lives as well. We go merrily along, thinking our speech and actions are covered with a protective tarmac of discretion, when suddenly a pernicious weed works its way to the surface. *Crabgrass* (complaining) pops right up, permeating our speech, or *henbit* (gossip) spreads its ugly tendrils into our neighbor's garden. Every time we fret, *knotweed* quickly sprouts and binds us, holding us hostage with anxiety. *Sandbur* (anger)—the most abrupt and relentless—irritates us until it shoots up and takes over, making even the most peaceful space a hotbed. *Hogweed* (envy and covetousness) is not only noxious but may be the granddaddy of them all.

Just when we think we've got our ground covered, we need to be on guard and watch for such besetting weeds in the garden of our thoughts, speech, and behavior. We need to humbly ask God, the Master Gardener, to help us be rid of them before they ruin the landscape of our lives.

A man's nature runs either to herbs, or to weeds; therefore let him seasonably water the one, and destroy the other

– Francis Bacon

Grace

To be
A lovely rose
Birthed on a thorny vine,
Unfolding grace to sun above,
Imparting fragrance sweet to earth below,
And kissed afresh by morning dew.
Such velvet love expressed!
If one could choose
To be.

Grace is the beauty of form under the influence of freedom

– Friedrich Schiller

Beholding the Beauty around Us

We've all done it. We are so intent upon a mission or so engrossed in our own little world that we miss much of what is present around us. Henry David Thoreau noted, "It's not what we look at that matters, it's what we see".

We pass a tree or a flower or another person without really seeing the beauty they possess. "Been there, seen that" is our ho-hum attitude. Oh, yes, we've all heard the admonition to "take time to smell the flowers" and we promise ourselves we will—tomorrow, perhaps, because we've too much to do today.

Sometimes when we give the slightest regard to a person or thing, it can make a difference—in them and in us. Many of us have heard the story "A Simple Gesture," about a bullied child who was on his way to commit suicide when someone befriended him. He said that small act of kindness made a decisive difference because it saved his life. Paying attention to people means seeing them as God sees them.

All He has created is unique and special. While typing these few lines, I've looked away long enough from the monitor to appreciate the splendor that I often overlook in my own backyard. Two butterflies visit the crimson hibiscus on the patio and a hummingbird hovers at our window feeder. As I consider the wonder of these amazing creatures, I take time to slow down and drink it in.

Emerson said it well: "Never lose an opportunity of seeing anything that is beautiful, for beauty is God's handwriting—a wayside sacrament. Welcome it in every fair face, in every sky, in every fair flower, and thank God for it as a cup of blessing."

. . . whatever things are lovely . . . think about these things

– Philippians 4:8

Lady of the Night

Only while you sleep
Do I lift my gaze
To golden moonbeam kisses
And open my arms
To gentle night breezes -
Welcoming their embrace

Only at nightfall
Do I bare my true essence
Unwrapping velvet robe
Dropping all pretense
Of hidden countenance -
Unmasking my radiant face

Only in dark night
Do I emit my fragrance
Bestowing perfume abroad
Sweet scent of blossoms
Bathing the air -
Infusing dusky space

Only at morning
Do I recoil and retreat
Quickly wrapping cloak
And veil around me
Yielding to the dawn -
Bidding adieu in grace

*Flowers that bloom only at night are like stars in the night sky —
evidence of God's promises even while our eyes are closed in sleep*

— Sandra Fischer

Happiness in Bloom

From azaleas to hydrangeas to crape myrtle, we see happiness in bloom all spring and summer on Dataw Island. The vivid colors gracing the landscape affect our emotions and state of mind. It's true; studies by Rutgers University show that flowers indeed make people happy.

In one group of several hundred women, all those who received flowers as a gift smiled, yet only seventy-seven percent of those who received candles did and only ten percent of those receiving fruit did. (I don't think they studied those who received chocolate).

Another study that included men proved the same. In fact, some scientists say the floral industry has evolved into growing things that serve no other purpose than emotional satisfaction. Terry McGuire, one of the Rutgers professors, says that "flowers are a source of pleasure, a positive emotion inducer—we take care of them and in that sense they are like dogs—our plant world 'pets,' so to speak."

Think of all the artists who in poem, song, or painting have extolled the loveliness of flowers, and how such renderings bless our homes and hearts. We have the same regard for flowers as butterflies do; we are attracted by their fragrance and sustained by drinking in their beauty. Robert Ingersoll said, "Every flower about a house certifies to the refinement of somebody. Every vine climbing and blossom tells of love and joy."

For the beauty of the earth—field and flower—let us give praise!

Flowers always make people better, happier, and more helpful;
they are sunshine, food and medicine to the soul

– Luther Burbank

Seeds of Sacrifice

Seeds give way to stems, stems give way to flowers, and flowers give way to seeds again. The process is a matter of small sacrifices in a cycle that allows the garden life to continue. Lives of people are constituted of the same giving ways—some by nature and some by choice.

Such was said of Todd Beamer who made the ultimate sacrifice on that infamous day in September, 2001. Todd was not one of the courageous firemen or police officers or emergency personnel who clamored to the awful scenes at the twin towers in New York and at the Pentagon in Washington and gave their lives in an effort to save those they could.

Todd Beamer was one of the men on Flight 93 who rushed the cockpit and overcame the terrorists before they could use that plane to kill and destroy another planned target. The plane crashed in a Pennsylvania field. Beamer and the others were lauded as heroes.

Later, Todd's widow, Lisa, said her husband was an ordinary man, and everything he did until 9/11 was preparing him for that day. He didn't suddenly decide to become a hero; he had been developing the character of one all along. He had been making "little sacrifices" all his life. While on 9/11 he gave his all, to Lisa, he was a hero by the way he had lived each and every day.

We may never be called to give our very lives in such a moment, but every day we have the opportunity to give of ourselves in ways that will bless others and transform us in the process. Each day we can show kindness instead of criticism, mercy instead of judgment, grace instead of begrudging, forbearance instead of selfishness, love instead of indifference. Our seeds of sacrifice can give way to stems of mercy, to flowers of grace, and to new seeds of life.

By this we know love, that He laid down his life for us, and we ought to lay down our lives for the brothers

– 1 John 3:16

Garden Ballerina

Poised in brilliant array,
She embodies elegant beauty -
Floating and fluttering
On feathery wings –
Gossamer canvases
Brushed in vivid color -
Intricately created
By the Divine Designer
To bless garden and soul.

In silent splendor
She dances on tiptoe
Across sun-drenched petals
Spreading her arms
In graceful symmetry.

Flowers embrace her
Children chase her
Enraptured men praise her.
She goes wherever she pleases
And pleases wherever she goes
An incomparable insect -
She neither bites nor stings
But kisses the earth
With delight and joy.

Butterflies are self-propelled flowers

– R.H. Heinlein

Hope's Sunrise Serenade

Some folks are awakened by a GE alarm that buzzes, others by the voice of a morning disc jockey on a Sony. I have a "Wren." Each morning before daybreak, the warble of this small bird brings me to consciousness, a gentle awareness that night has passed and morning has come.

A new day, a new chance, and a clean slate await me as I consider the hope expressed in the bird's song. To some, this trilling isn't so thrilling at such an early hour, but it's a wonderful way to greet a new day. To begin the morn with a song is an expression of gratitude, a melody of potential and promise. It's an announcement to the world: "Hey, I'm still here—another day to live, to be, to sing."

Of course, some people don't readily burst into song when their feet hit the floor nor appreciate the sound of music in the morning nor greet the day with expectation. The alarm that many times startles them into consciousness may garner a negative response: "Beware, look out, another day is here!"

The difference may be in our heart attitude toward life. If we listen with gratitude and grasp how precious a present God has given us each morning, the wren is accepted as God's messenger. This little songbird is a sweet reminder of how blessed we are by the same Creator.

Sometimes as I listen to the morning serenade, a refrain will press into my consciousness. *This is the day, this is the day that the Lord hath made,* or *When morning gilds the skies, my heart awaking cries, may Jesus Christ be praised.* When this happens, I find myself eager to see what God has planned for me. My hope for the new day is the assurance that He is already there working out every detail in His plan and purpose for me. I need not be alarmed into the awareness that a new day has dawned nor of what it may bring.

The wren's sunrise serenade is one of true hope, not wishful thinking. Perhaps its melodious sound is what inspired Emily Dickinson to write:

"Hope" is the thing with feathers -
That perches in the soul -
And sings the tune without the words -
And never stops – at all -

Thanks, little wren, for your morning call—for filling the air with the song God gave you. May it instill my heart with the same praise music to His faithful providence.

The steadfast love of the LORD never ceases; his mercies never come to an end; they are new every morning; great is your faithfulness

– Lamentations 3:22-23

Of Times and Seasons

Days are dwindling shorter now,
Summer's winding down.
Autumn's new décor is here -
Orange, gold, and brown.

Butterflies dance their last dance,
Leaves kiss trees goodbye.
Birds that once were fledglings
Soar across the sky.

The vine has given forth its fruit,
Nuts fall on the ground.
Hummingbirds will soon pack up
And flurry out of town.

It may seem sad to bid farewell
To summer's golden glow,
Yet God in all His wisdom
Planned an ebb and flow.

Each season's blessed with attributes
We relish when it's here,
Then like another birthday,
It passes every year.

Our lives – like passing seasons
We greet, then bid adieu,
Yet Hope holds forth the promise -
The old will yield to new.

So say goodbye to summer days
And welcome in the fall.
Be grateful for each season
Wrought – the wonder of them all.

While the earth remains,
seedtime and harvest,
cold and heat,
summer and winter,
day and night,
shall not cease.

– Genesis 8:22

Fall

No spring nor summer beauty hath such grace
As I have seen in one autumnal face.

John Donne

FALL IS FULL of vibrant changing colors, appearing like a patchwork quilt thrown over the landscape. Purples, reds, oranges, and golds gradually appear on tree and ground. Skies take on a more intense blue as days grow shorter, and stars become more visible on crisp, clear nights. Temperatures moderate and humidity lessens as cooler winds begin to sweep in and thunderstorms abate. Fall is settling in.

People and beasts both gather the fruit of the harvest, celebrate its blessings, and store up resources for the coming winter season. Birds and butterflies begin their southward migration, and the sun seems to follow as the earth slowly rotates. Some animals don winter coats to withstand the coming cold, while others prepare to hibernate.

To the naked eye, it appears that all flora is dying—while in reality, seeds are being scattered and bulbs are forming in the ground. All bear a promise of renewal and birth come spring.

We see parallels of the autumn season of humanity as displayed in our advancing years. We begin to slowly settle into a time of mellowing, a season of celebrating and enjoying the fruit of our labors. Time is spent reflecting about the past and sharing the wisdom we have gleaned from it with anyone who will listen. We realize we are approaching the latter season of life. Our bodies begin to sag and wrinkle, much like the leaves on trees. The specter of winter is on the horizon.

Like nature, we also scatter seed as the legacies we leave to those who follow us. Family mementos and traditions are passed along, entrusted to posterity to keep and cherish them. We sense that what we leave in the hearts of our children is more lasting than what we leave in their hands.

Autumn is Come

Autumn is come, unannounced,
Subtly drifting in on cool cloud wings
Blotting out the scorch of summer.

Gowned in golden melancholy,
Robes streaming ruby and scarlet
She spreads her garment abroad
On field grass and marsh reed
Transforming each blade and stalk
And our memory of what once was green.

Bearing fruit, she bids the harvester
"Come, eat, drink – the yield of seed
And labor have come full measure.
My vines are heavy; my limbs bowed low -
I come to fill, sustain, and give,
To be refreshed to give again."

Gladly we revel in Autumn's bounty,
Grateful for the blessed increase
She bears – abundance arrayed
On a platter of irresistible bronze beauty.
We bask in the joy of her company,
Content with her presence, until. . .

On cue, leaves shrivel, shiver, and give way
To the Master's plan for *all* seasons;
Autumn is, but is not everything.

For everything there is a season, and a time for every matter under heaven

– Ecclesiastes 3:1

Flower Children

Some gardeners treat their flowers like children: giving them special attention as they're budding, feeding them a proper diet, staking them when they need support, and praising them when they blossom. Consider, too, how children are like flowers. They come in a wide variety of shapes, sizes, and colors. Their personalities are distinct—some are shy like violets, while others, like sunflowers, put on a big show. Still others may display all kinds of stubbornness, choosing to branch out into risky areas.

Some children are self-starters; they seem to adapt themselves easily and thrive even in the most adverse conditions. And of course, some are like fragile orchids, requiring extra attention and care. Most children—and flowers—will flourish when nurtured in the best possible environment, one that produces just the right balance of love and discipline to keep them healthy. Too much sun or shelter can inhibit them from gaining true maturity. Ever notice those who are like lily buds that don't open and never reach their full potential? And there are those who still have a lackadaisical attitude, not caring whether they produce anything noteworthy.

All children need to be protected from weedy and buggy predators that hang around even the most cultured neighborhoods. Asking for some Divine intervention is the best idea in overseeing the whole process; after all, gardening and children were God's ideas. Most of all, children need to be well-rooted, knowing how their lives have been perpetuated by a legacy of seeds planted through generations. They need to appreciate the heritage they possess for future gardens, so the world will continue to be blessed with beautiful "flower children."

Train up a child in the way he should go; even he is old he will not depart from it

– Proverbs 22:6 (ESV)

In Galaxies and Gardens – A Sense of Place

Have you ever noticed stars punctuating a crisp, clear autumn night? They are like innumerable bits of glitter shimmering on black velvet. Scientists can only estimate their number at something like 70 sextillion—ten times more, it is said, than the grains of sand on our beaches and deserts. When considering that Earth's sun is only *one* such star, we get a humbling perspective of our place in the vast universe.

As a young shepherd, David spent many nights stargazing and many days writing poetry that acknowledges our modest state by saying to God: "When I consider your heavens, the work of your fingers . . . what is man that you are mindful of him?"

Yet when life began in earth's green garden, humanity's position relative to the rest of the world was one of stature, and David notes that as he continues Psalm 8. "You made him ruler ... you put everything under his feet." What a different view this gives of our place in the realm of earthly things as appointed by God.

How should we view ourselves? Of relative insignificance or as someone special? By the position God has given us on earth, some of us become very aware of our earthly nature, while others are enamored with our heavenly nature. We need both perspectives in life to have a balanced picture of who we are in the whole scheme, and to realize our sense of place in both galaxies and gardens.

Lift up your eyes and look to the heavens:
Who created all these?
He who brings out the starry host one by one
and calls forth each of them by name.
Because of his great power and mighty strength,
not one of them is missing

– Isaiah 40:26

Going to School in the Garden

Who would imagine the garden to be a school—a sort of "Green Thumb University?" It's a wonderful learning center for willing students, and not just for horticultural lessons one can learn about where to plant what and when, or how to get the best yield. Rather, it's a training center with life lessons sprouting up and taking root in us as we ponder principles for living found in the gardening process.

My father, an avid, successful gardener, demonstrated how every good garden produces not only peas, but "P's" … in the gardener. He showed the "P" of *Patience*—the necessary character trait of waiting for seeds to germinate, emerge, and grow into adult plants. Patience is based on the principle of delayed gratification—that good things come to those who wait.

A second "P" in the garden school is *Perseverance*—a steadfast spirit in tending the garden with wisdom and care. Perseverance is protecting against the severity of circumstances: drought, wind, weeds, and pests. Learning to persevere helps us to prevail over life's circumstances, instead of being plowed under by them.

Finally, a third "P" is *Perspiration.* I never met a true gardener who didn't sweat, and who didn't relish the relationship of diligent labor to success. Nobody plows a garden by turning it over in their mind. The fruit produced by toil tastes the sweetest, or as the book of Proverbs teaches, "All hard work brings a profit" (Proverbs 14:23 NIV).

The garden is a great place to go to school, whether to get a "Green Thumb" degree or to get a degree of "Thumbs-up" in life learning.

Let perseverance finish its work so that you may be mature and complete, not lacking anything

– James 1:4 (NIV)

The CSN Club

Walking past a blooming rose in her garden, a woman promised to return, cut it, and take it to a terminally ill friend, but she allowed busyness with other things to swallow up her good intentions. Two days later, she remembered and returned to the garden to find the rose spent, its petals lying on the ground. That same day she learned that her friend had died.

At the funeral, she and another friend stood at the casket, listening to many glowing compliments spoken of the deceased. *Too late*, she thought.

She touched the arm of the friend beside her and looked into her eyes. "I want to tell you *now* how much you mean to me. I want you to know what a blessing you are in my life."

From that day forward, the woman promised herself she would not let a day pass without taking the opportunity to thank or praise someone in word or deed. She invited others to join her in what could be called the "CSN (Compliment Someone Now) Club."

Anyone can join this club. There are no age requirements and no dues. Meetings are held at the members' discretion—whenever they meet someone and choose to call the meeting to order by offering a kind remark. The only bylaw is to not let a day go by without complimenting someone. The effect can make a difference in someone's day—or even longer. Mark Twain said, "I can live for two months on a good compliment."

Anytime is a good time to join the CSN Club and to take the opportunity to shower others with kind words and acts of appreciation.

A single act of kindness throws out roots in all directions, and the roots spring up and make new trees
– Amelia Earhart

A Harvest of Blessing

Gardeners look forward to harvest time when they can take pleasure in seeing the results of their labor. Flower and fruit have matured upon the vine while vegetables buried beneath the soil are ready to be uncovered like hidden treasures. Sometimes the harvest can bring lost treasures to light, as it did to one gardener.

Many years ago, I read a story about an elderly woman and her husband who were devoted to a wonderful vegetable garden they had cared for over many years. When her husband died, she offered to let her neighbor treat the garden as if it were his. At harvest time, the neighbor was digging carrots from it when he suddenly stopped to examine one that had an unusual shape. It seemed to have grown into an hourglass figure, wide at the top and bottom, but very narrow at the center. As he brushed the dirt off the carrot, he was shocked at what he found in its middle—a gold ring! Somehow, the root vegetable had grown all around and through the ring.

Inside the ring, he found a date inscribed, indicating the ring was fifty years old. He took it to the widow. Her mouth dropped as she took it in her hand, and tears streamed down her face.

"This is my wedding ring. My husband gave it to me the day we married and I was most grieved when I lost it a few years ago. We were blessed to celebrate our 50th anniversary just before he passed this spring. How special for God to uncover it in the place we held so dear—it's a harvest blessing."

If we look, we too can find a harvest in places all around us: treasure in the dirt, light in the darkness, blessings in unexpected places. God has mysterious ways of showing His providential care just when we need it most.

The earth has yielded its increase; God, our God, shall bless us

– Psalm 67:6

Familiar Birds of a Feather

I am an avid birdwatcher, fascinated by the habits and antics of feathered friends as they go about their daily routines. I've noticed that some of their behavior is similar to human actions.

Take the nuthatch, for example. He goes to the feeder, selects a piece of seed, and then flies to a tree to hide it so that he can enjoy it later. I've known some closet cookie eaters who hide food from other family members so they will be sure to have some for themselves later. A problem can occur, however, if (like me), they can't remember where they hid it.

Then there are the blue jays, well known for making their noisy approach and clearing the smaller birds out of their way. I've met some of these birds on the highway and at potlucks—fast lane changers who cut me off and buffet butt-in-skis who elbow their way through the food line.

The male cardinal is also interesting. He takes seed in his mouth and feeds it to his mate. This puzzles me, because somehow, this habit has been reversed in the human counterpart, at least in some households. I seem to hear, "Honey, while you're up, would you bring me a whatever-it-is?" The remedy may be to stay put until he gets up.

And then there's the mockingbird—talk about the king of peer pressure! I notice lots of mockingbirds in our neighborhood flying around; most of them do everything they can to keep up with whatever the latest trend may be—the latest model car or tech upgrade.

When people say life is for the birds, it may be because their behavior can resemble that of some feathered creatures. While I have seen some resemblances, I'm reminded, too, of how God cares for all those He has made.

Look at the birds of the air; they neither sow nor reap nor gather into barns, and yet your heavenly Father feeds them

– Matthew 6:26

The "Bubba Gump" Cure

Part of the wonderful experience when we moved from northern Indiana to Dataw Island, South Carolina was discovering and enjoying the perennial flora and fauna indigenous to the Low Country. Yet when October came around, I suffered from nostalgic "apple fever." As a transplant from Johnny Appleseed's backyard, I missed the orchards and the pioneer festivals that celebrate the harvest of this delectable member of the rose family. I yearned for the aroma of apple butter simmering in giant copper kettles, the taste of hot apple fritters, the rich aroma of spicy apple cider brewed over open flames, and the fascinating sight of dried apple-headed figures fashioned into dolls. Yes, I knew I could buy apples at the local market, but wasn't the same as picking them fresh from a tree and taking a peck home to make applesauce and pie.

The good news is that I have found the remedy for such melancholy. I call it the "Bubba Gump" cure, a shrimp prescription for apple doldrums. Here in South Carolina, I have shrimp caught fresh from the coastal waters nearby, ready to make shrimp cocktail, shrimp gumbo, shrimp scampi, shrimp 'n' grits, shrimp salad—just a few of the delicious renditions from Bubba Gump's exhaustive list. My southern backyard is a virtual sea orchard, brimming with such fruit to be netted and savored. When I catch a whiff of shrimp-kabobs roasting on the grill, the memory of apple dumplings quickly fades. It reminds me that when we relinquish something in life, we can either bemoan its absence or accept and even embrace its replacement.

So goodbye to fresh-picked apples and hello to fresh-caught shrimp.

Not that I am speaking of being in need, for I have learned in whatever situation I am to be content

– Philippians 4:11

October on Stage

The morning sun cries, "Curtain Up!"
On this golden autumn day -
A drama posed with many scenes
In life's unfolding play.

The ever-changing set reveals
A bright October sky,
Backdrops painted brilliant blue
As whipped cream clouds pile high.

Marsh reed tips are flaxen now and
Leaf curls etched with brown
Soon will fall confetti-like
On actors bowing down.

Confederate Rose – October's star -
Enters right on cue,
Her first blooms – white with innocence -
Her next – a pale pink hue.

You crown the year
with your bounty;
your wagon tracks
overflow with abundance

– Psalm 65:11

How like the landscapes fleeting by -
Swift seasons, days and hours,
She sings and dances through the scene
In costume-changing flowers.

In Act Three, she's magenta – bold -
Full blossomed, flaming red,
Then, like a crimson sunset, bids
"Good night" and goes to bed.

The stage is dark – the curtain falls;
The day has had its run
Yet hearts applaud the splendid show -
A glorious play – well done!

It's the Great Pumpkin...

Fall harvest time in the garden means a variety of fruits and vegetables. Apples are one of the most prominent, but nothing says *fall* like pumpkins. These round, versatile and fascinating squash proliferate on our doorsteps as decorations and on our tables as food.

Ordinarily we think of these golden orbs as rather limited in scope and purpose. But take a closer look—pumpkins come in many colors, including blue and white, and their uses are not limited to jack-o'-lanterns and pie. Cookbooks are replete with recipes for everything from fried pumpkin blossoms to roasted pumpkin seeds to stir-fried pumpkin vines, not to mention the brew early American settlers made—pumpkin beer.

Nutritionists tout the healthy aspects of pumpkin seeds and pulp; they are low in calories and sodium, while high in protein, iron, B vitamins, and beta-carotene. The shells can be used for more than carving jack-o'-lanterns. Native Americans dried the shells and wove mats from them, while today many people use them as serving bowls for soups, stews, and dips.

October is a time to rejoice in what Charlie Brown's friend, Linus, yearned for every year and what we may just take for granted—perhaps the most

Prolific, Unique, Magnificent Produce Known In Nature

Pumpkins, like all God's creation, have within them seeds of possibilities

– Sandra Fischer

Late Bloomers

Having retired and moved to South Carolina from the Midwest, where flower-growing seasons were shortened by Jack Frost's arrival, I delight in seeing what some there would call *late bloomers*. Black-eyed susans, bittersweet, mums, and asters—all are spurred on by a more temperate climate to grace the southern landscape with lively color. They continue to emerge and blossom late into the year.

Flowers aren't the only ones that bloom late; some people are known to be late bloomers as well. Grandma Moses didn't start painting until she was seventy, Colonel Sanders didn't cook up that chicken franchise idea until he was past sixty. Laura Ingalls Wilder was over sixty when she published her first novel.

As I look around the community where we've retired, I notice artists, photographers, writers, craftsmen, and entrepreneurs budding with creative energy. Many are in their golden years and have taken up these avocations with relish. These late bloomers seem to have found the right combination of a pleasant, inspirational climate and the soil of encouragement that allows them to flourish. Much like the flowers that lend beauty late into the season, they enrich the lives of those around them.

The righteous flourish like the palm tree and grow like a cedar of Lebanon. They are planted in the house of the LORD; they flourish in the courts of our God. They still bear fruit in old age they are ever full of sap and green

– Psalm 92:12-14

Flowery Friends

It has been said that friends are the flowers in life's garden. I agree, because I see characteristics in my friends that are reflected in various flowers.

One of my friends is a daisy—cheerful, bright, and perky. Rarely does anything upset her or keep her from having a positive attitude. Another is a violet—a good listener, quiet and unobtrusive, yet always there to stand alongside. She might not be noticed in a crowd, but her demeanor is one of perceptive assurance.

My daffodil chum lends a sunny perspective with her contagious smiles and giggles. She stands right up to be noticed and trumpets her opinion to those who are willing to give her space.

And who can keep secrets better than my mum buddy? Her beauty does not belie her trustworthiness. She's a perennial staple in any garden. Oh, yes, I do have an impatiens too, who can be a little demanding now and then, but she may have been placed in my life to teach me the importance of forbearance.

Magnolia, who seems to weather most difficulties with aplomb, displays strength of character. Little fazes her; she just blossoms in the face of whatever storms may come.

My sweet pea is a friend who is thoughtful, caring, always thinking of others and how she can show compassion. And my bittersweet friend is the opposite—her mood swings counterbalance the landscape with life's ups and downs and how easily they affect her.

Perhaps the most faithful in my friendship garden is a rose, ever-blossoming with kindness, gentleness, and forgiveness. She even blooms in winter when others have become dormant or have left the garden.

Each friend is unique and special, just as is every flower in a garden. As I gather thoughts of them, I realize how they become a beautiful bouquet, adding fragrance and beauty on my pathway of life.

Friends are like flowers that brighten your day,
With fragrance and beauty to share on life's way.
So treat them like flowers from the Gardener above;
Weed them with mercy and water with love

— Author Unknown

Observing the Month of Thanksgiving

Notice how each day is
Only as special as the
View of those who
Esteem its gifts, who
Make it count
By reverberating its
Extraordinary
Rewards in humble gratitude

Every good gift and every perfect gift is from above, coming down from the Father of lights with whom there is no variation or shadow due to change

– James 1:17

Celebrating November

As we come to celebrate the month of November, we usually think only of the two days most associated with it: Veteran's Day and Thanksgiving. Traditionally, these special holidays are set aside, but if we want to celebrate more than these two special days, we can find an extended list of activities and events assigned to November. Such interesting titles attributed to the whole month include "Adopt a Turkey" and "Sweet Potato Awareness," while "National Fig Week" and "Better Conversation Week" are set aside as remarkable week-long observances.

Designations don't stop there either. Every day of November has been labeled with something, from "Plan your Epitaph Day" to one that is more appealing to me—"National Men Make Dinner Day." Over one hundred unique names are distributed among November's thirty days, yet I found only one special day remotely related to gardening—"National Pickle Day."

Perhaps our Dataw Garden Club could expand recognition in this area by suggesting several titles for November based on the beauty in our own backyards. We could add 'Butterfly Garden Day,' 'Confederate Rose Day,' and 'Sasanqua Camellia Day,' just for starters.

To recognize the kind of community we have here on Dataw Island, we could also propose setting aside a 'Garden of Friends Day,' a 'Blooming Hospitality Island Day,' or a "Harvest of Good Things Day.' But those would actually bring us back to the one day we can commemorate every day—Thanksgiving.

Whether we want to celebrate turkeys or sweet potatoes or figs or pickles or the community in which we live, we can simply do so by observing Thanksgiving, whether it's November or not. We can be grateful for our many blessings every day, wherever we are planted.

This is the day that the Lord has made;
let us rejoice and be glad in it

– Psalm 118:24

Gathering and Scattering

Thanksgiving is a wonderful compound word with two kernels of meaning. It's not just about expressing thanks—that's only half. It's also about giving to demonstrate our thankfulness. It's sharing the bounty of blessings we enjoy, an overflow of gratitude for what we have. It's scattering what we've gathered.

All of us are familiar with the history of the holiday, but some may not know that the tradition was not begun the first year after the Pilgrims arrived. Following their first harsh winter in 1621, the Pilgrims resorted to food rationing to survive. According to legendary accounts, each person was allotted a mere five grains of corn per day, for which they still gave thanks. Two years later, after a plentiful harvest, tradition says they celebrated the first Thanksgiving.

Eventually, Thanksgiving Day was set aside in remembrance. As we celebrate the holiday, we might consider giving each person five kernels of corn and asking them to give thanks for a blessing in their life for each grain of corn, a reminder of God's provision.

In addition, we might ask each to consider how their grains of corn could be scattered in gratitude for their blessings.

In 2011, Chilean miners stranded underground did just that. They rationed their food and water and gave thanks for the smallest of provisions, keeping a true perspective of what is important and sacred—life and liberty. They scattered what they had gathered.

Our history and their example should remind us that giving is the kernel of true Thanksgiving. Spreading abroad our gratitude is the overflow of our blessings

You will be enriched in every way to be generous in every way, which through us will produce thanksgiving to God

– 2 Corinthians 9:11

A Cardinal's Song and True Thanksgiving

Have you ever noticed that a cardinal's song sounds like a question—*what cheer?* Their beautiful red coat belies the fact that they appear to be searching for some happiness around the birdfeeder. It might remind us of someone we know—someone who gives the appearance that all is well, but underneath their feathers lurks discontent. Some people remind me of that questioning red bird. They think they would be happier if they just had more time or money or whatever it is they believe would fulfill their lives or change their situations. Some think life would be better if they *didn't* have some of the things they do.

The key is in realizing just how blessed we are, regardless of circumstances or possessions. My friend, Becky Guinn, is a great example. She counts every day a blessing as she faces daily challenges, never complaining that she is doing it with two artificial arms and two artificial legs. She is happy to be alive and to be doing what she loves. Since losing her limbs several years ago, Becky has transformed the cardinal's song from a question to an exclamation—*what cheer!*—as she continues to render beautiful artwork with a mechanical hand. She expresses gratitude instead of discontent, because the joy of the Lord is her strength. Her faith in God has sustained her through her life and its challenges as she has learned to rely on Him.

Perhaps the secret to true thanksgiving and contentment is not in having what we want, but in wanting what we have. Trusting in God's provision regardless of the circumstances is a lesson we can learn to apply in our lives if we want the peace that passes all understanding.

. . . for I have learned in whatever situation I am to be content. . .In any and every circumstance, I have learned the secret of facing plenty and hunger, abundance and need. I can do all things through Him who strengthens me

– Philippians 4:11-13

Thanksgiving Recipe

(Main Course)
Taken from the cookbook Joy of Heavenly Cooking

Select 18 lbs. (or more) of Blessings
Stuff with Gratitude
Season with Kindred Broth
Roast with the Warmth of Humor
Baste with the Oil of Kind Words
Serve on a Platter of Goodwill
Carve some Savory Memories
Pass the Gravy of Compliments
Ladle lavishly with Love
Taste the Flavor of Fellowship
Enjoy a Hearty Feast of Grace
All from the hand of God

And whatever you do, in word or deed, do everything in the name of the Lord Jesus, giving thanks to God the Father through him

– Colossians 3:17

Grandma's Gratitude Quilt

Grandma made a patchwork quilt
Of remnants cut from life –
Parts of Grandpa's work shirts,
Denim blue like skies
On plowing days and harvest
Thank you, Lord, for the bounty

Blocks of rose and brown
Cut from her calico apron
Washed clean of sweet aromas
Thank you, Lord, for sustenance

Poplin flowered squares
Plotted like pink peonies picked
From Grandma's garden
Thank you, Lord, for beauty

Checked gingham triangles –
Material from a doll's dress
Fashioned for a child's delight
Thank you, Lord, for joy

Pillow ticking borders
Binding them all together -
Bits and pieces of kinship
Thank you, Lord, for family

We will not hide them
from their children,
but tell to the coming generation,
the glorious deeds of the LORD,
and his might,
and the wonders that He has done

– Psalm 78:4

The fabric of lives spread over years
Covering, comforting, blessing me
Under the warmth of memories
Tucked in the recesses of my heart
Stitched with threads of love
Thank you, Lord, for Grandma's patchwork quilt

Thanksgiving Squashed?

November means jacket weather, pansy planting, harvest moons, and Thanksgiving. Unfortunately, this holiday seems lost in the shuffle, squashed between trick-or-treating and Christmas. One may find a few paper turkeys or cornucopia decorations among row upon row of Halloween costumes and Christmas decorations (available earlier each year), but attention to Thanksgiving is brief. It's relegated to a hurried celebration piled high with food, family, and football.

What distinguishes this holiday is the fact that it was not begun in honor of an individual or group or symbol. Thanksgiving began as an attitude toward life. Based on the oldest celebration in our country's history, it's an exemplary event started by the Pilgrims who came to this land in hopes of finding fertile soil for planting seeds of freedom. They suffered hardships and losses, yet on a day centuries ago, they shared a meager meal of a few corn kernels and thanked God for what they had. We, who now dwell in this free land teeming with abundance and opportunity, can do no less than they did by counting and sharing our blessings.

Let's take time to make more thoughtful preparations for Thanksgiving each year and to give it more regard than squashing it between other holidays. And may our leftovers be more than "talking turkey"; rather, may they be an overflow of grateful expressions we share with one another all year long.

Bless the LORD, O my soul, and forget not all his benefits

– Psalm 103:2

The Lesson of the Blessing Box

A wise teacher gave a box to each of two sisters, telling them, "This is a blessing box; use the blessings well." Each box had a lid with two hands embossed on it, both with palms turned upward, and each contained three items: a flower, a gold coin, and a bird's egg.

The sisters were to keep their boxes for a week and return to the teacher to share how they had used the blessings. When they returned with their boxes at the end of the week, the teacher asked each sister to tell what she had done with the contents.

Blessing Box

The first girl opened hers to show the flower, pressed and dried. She had kept the gold coin and bird's egg. She told the teacher how blessed she had been by the loveliness and fragrance of the flower, so she dried it to keep. The coin she hoped to redeem for an object she wanted to buy and the bird's egg was so pretty, she wanted it as a remembrance of the beauty of birds.

The second girl opened her box. It was empty. The teacher asked, "Did you not receive the same as your sister—a flower, a coin, and a bird's egg?"

"Yes," she said, "I received them, but they were too precious to keep. I took the seed from the flower and planted it, so more flowers might grow. I gave the coin to a poor neighbor who had none, and I returned the egg to its mother's nest so it could hatch."

The teacher said, "My child, you have wisely used the blessing box as illustrated by the two hands on the lid. When we open one hand to receive a blessing, then open the other to pass it on, the blessing is multiplied. That is why God has given us two hands—one to receive and one to give."

One gives freely, yet grows all the richer; another withholds what he should give,
and only suffers want. Whoever brings blessing will be enriched,
and one who waters will himself be watered

– Proverbs 11:24-25

Steps to Peace

The world has all kinds of 'step' programs to help us in times of need: exercise step programs, 12-step programs, 'one step at a time' programs—but for us who have a garden, we are only one step away from entering a place where we can find serenity in a natural setting. Studies have shown that spending time in a garden can bring peace to troubles souls. The garden is a tonic for everyone who lives in this fragmented, frazzled world today.

So...

When we watch the news and hear of disasters everywhere—loss of jobs, loss of homes, loss of security, loss of life—and we are weary, we can...

Step into the garden and see new growth and beauty that does not strive, but rests in the Master Gardener's hands.

When our son or daughter calls to say they're getting a divorce and we hear the children crying and our hearts are breaking, too, we can ...

Step into the garden and take hope. We can see the renewal of life, each tender branch, leaf, and flower trusting in what only God can do to restore and nourish.

When we get the call from the doctor who says, "Yes, the tests are positive," and fear wraps its tendrils around our souls, we can ...

Step into the garden and breathe in the assurance that the One who planted the first perfect garden will tend us as He does each rose that grows on a thorny vine.

All that we have strived to make and build can be whisked away in a moment of fire or storm or neglect, but gardens have lasted since life on earth began. To find a sense of peace, serenity, and what is eternal, we can...

Step into the garden and rejoice.

Come to me, all who labor and are heavy laden, and I will give you rest

– Matthew 11:28

Winter

In seed-time learn, in harvest teach, in winter enjoy

William Blake

REST AND RECOVERY are the attributes of nature in winter. Flora and fauna alike retreat into dormant cycles, feeding on what has been stored for the seasonal time. Tree limbs are barren, animals are hibernating, grass has suspended growth—all are conserving energy during this time of cold temperatures and food scarcity. The process of rest and recovery are necessary parts of the seasonal cycle as each form of life prepares for regeneration.

So it is with mankind. Our winter season is full of rest and recovery as we preserve energy. We remember and process what we have learned, and we seek to pass that legacy of knowledge to those who will follow us. While our bodies may show the results of aging, our spirits within are filled with the seeds of promise given by God. We sense an eternal spring is coming—a future hope. Like the seed in the ground that yields itself to something new, the spirit of mankind yields to something more. We perceive that all seasons were made for us, and God, who made both them and us, takes pleasure in each one.

The Arbor Day Legacy

Shortly after we moved to the South Carolina Low Country, our new neighbor's mother died. We wanted to give something living in her memory, so we gave a Savannah holly seedling, which our neighbor planted between our properties. Each day we enjoy the stunning beauty of that tree, now standing over thirty feet tall and laden with brilliant red berries. It's particularly appropriate in December, as it's already decorated with red and green for Christmas.

Planting trees is a wonderful way to multi-task. We can plant them in honor or memory of someone, or simply as our gift in gratitude for all the things trees provide us. At the same time, we replenish the earth with beautiful foliage, and we invest in the future. Arbor Day, a day dedicated for tree planting, was started in 1872 when one man saw the need to plant trees in Nebraska as wind-breaks on the prairie. The idea grew (as well as the trees) and Arbor Day was proclaimed in each state.

The dates of Arbor Day vary by state according to the best time to plant a tree in the state's particular growing zone. South Carolina's Arbor Day falls in December, but no matter when the special day falls where we live, it's an opportunity to continue this living legacy. Arbor Day marks the beginning of the planting season, and it demonstrates the importance of all trees in our lives, whether they grow in the prairie, the mountains, or the Low Country.

"Arbor Day," said J. Sterling Morton, who started the idea, "is not like other holidays. Each of these reposes on the past, but Arbor Day *proposes* on the future."

Thomas Fuller, an English historian, noted, "He that plants trees loves others beside himself." Why not show that love by planting a tree on Arbor Day? It's a gift that keeps on living.

The earth brought forth vegetation, plants yielding seed according to their own kinds, and trees bearing fruit in which is their seed, each according to its kind. And God saw that it was good

– Genesis 1:12

A Tribute to Young Flowers

Flowers of earth's seasons
Hold their lifetime within
Some dying all too soon
By the gust of an evil blight -
And how we grieve their passing

But God
Has promises hidden deep
Within the legacies of flowers
Giving consolation to all
In every season – hope –

The surface of a dark December
Shows only barren landscapes
Brown and shriveled
Seemingly bereft by heartless
Wicked winter winds

But God
Makes everything beautiful
In time, stirring restless
Hidden kernels in the earth
To emerge forth in light
Of a new year's promises

The brief beauty of young flowers
Lives on in our heart's memory
While we envision how their
Spirits blossom eternally in heaven -
And we who remain wait patiently for
What Spring will surely bring.

He has made everything beautiful in its time.

– Ecclesiastes 3:11a

December Roses of Remembrance

There's a December rose in my garden. To some, it may be an anomaly, but it reminds me that December and roses have something in common—they bring remembrance. December is a time when families and friends gather, greetings are shared and memories of holidays past are recalled. Eyes glisten with recollections of ones who are absent, yet like the fragrance of the rose, they live on in our hearts long after they are gone.

We think of days when we were wide-eyed children struck by the wonder of the season. Like the warm glow of lighted candles, these memories permeate the shadows of December, dispelling the reality of another year passing. They become the special treasures found when we unwrap pleasant memories, gifts of the heart, to recall and to share with one another. We open them as we might the petals of a rose, to release their perfume into the present moment.

Sweet memories are ever-blooming flowers, and when they appear in the cold, wintry days of our lives, they bring comfort and the eternal hope that doesn't disappoint. In each present moment, we should be mindful that we are in the process of making memories—planting seeds of future Decembers.

God gave His children memory that in life's garden there might be June roses in December

– Rev. Geoffrey Anketall Studdert-Kennedy

Avoiding the Seasonal Bug

Ever notice during the holiday season how many people develop that seasonal malady called *holiday hysteria?*

Symptoms: Chills from shopping for that person on our list who has everything; fever brought on by overspending our budget; shortness of breath from running all over to find this year's most popular toy; headaches from wondering how we'll ever get all the shopping, wrapping, cleaning, cooking, card-writing, decorating, partying, visiting, pageant-attending, package-mailing, and gift-exchanging done.

What's the cure? I suppose we could take an extended trip far, far away, or make a declaration that we are skipping the tradition of Christmas gifts. A better way may be to plan and prioritize. You could ...

Stop and consider the reason the season is celebrated—how love came down in the form of a child and how Christ gave lasting gifts that meet deeper needs. Think about giving "heartmade" gifts—ones chosen with thought and care. For the person who has everything, "adopt" a needy child from in that person's name and give the child a gift instead. Or support an organization such as Samaritan's Purse that provides necessities to those who are not materially blessed. Write your children or grandchildren a keepsake letter about your childhood and your hopes for them—guaranteed to outlast any toy.

Choose to do only those activities that will be meaningful to you and others. The world will not stop if you do not attend all the parties and pageants. Plan to host your own parties during a different month of the year.

Instead of spending time at the mall, give that time to someone who needs a personal touch. Visit a relative in the nursing home or someone there who has no family coming to visit, or call on a shut-in in your neighborhood.

By prioritizing and planning, you can enjoy the season and avoid the *holiday hysteria* bug. Taking charge of our own healthy approach to the Christmas season will ensure *holiday heartiness* instead, and will be a blessing to you and to those on whom you bestow your heartmade gifts.

The heart of Christmas is love – love in action ~

This Place is for the Birds

Each year Dataw Island participates in the South Carolina Christmas Bird Count. On a special weekend in December, a list of our feathered friends is sent to island residents, and we are asked to record the species and numbers we see anywhere on the island and report them. As I set about to participate, I made some sightings of similar two-legged creatures befitting some of the names of the birds on the list.

At the Community Center, a few *Painted Buntings* were creating canvases for the Visual Arts Club. Across the hall were eight *Cardinals* at two tables, playing bridge. Down the hall were six *Warblers,* singing along as they kept in step with Dancercise music. I saw six *Thrashers* in the indoor pool, making waves with their water aerobics.

At the marina, I watched a couple of *Boat-tailed Grackles* docking their yachts, and a *Kingfisher* throwing out a baited line from his pier. Later, I counted two *Skimmers* kayaking on Jenkins Creek.

The golf driving range boasted many *Bald Eagles*, a couple of *Buffleheads* and a *Mockingbird* trying to replicate Tiger Woods' swing. I observed three *Chipping Sparrows* nearby trying to make some chip-ins, and a *Rough-legged Hawk* in red shorts lining up a putt on the practice green.

At the pub, several *Sapsuckers* were celebrating someone's hole-in-one. I assume it was made by the *American Crow,* who kept carrying on about it while buying drinks for the house.

There were one or two *Snowy Egrets* on the croquet lawn, and I heard a *Screech Owl* on the tennis court, who undoubtedly had just double-faulted. A *Swan* was considering a dive into the outdoor pool, but fortunately changed its mind, as the cover was still on.

A whole flock of Garden Club *Chickadees*, too many to count, were meeting in the Carolina Room, chirping about their winter gardens. As I headed home, I saw two *Roadrunners* jogging around the island circle.

All in all, I found very few *Grouse* and only one old *Coot.* I could tell from the fascinating ones I counted that the birds who live here are as happy as *Larks,* and they consider their surroundings to make them *Birds of Paradise.*

Beside them the birds of the heavens dwell; they sing among the branches

– Psalm 104:12

Living Luminarias

Every year, the Dataw Island Garden Club holds "Light up the Night," a luminaria celebration that brings a radiance to the island neighborhood each December. Those who participate by lining their driveways with candle lights in paper bags create a magical aura. The luminarias are like bits of sprinkled stars on the landscape, setting the island aglow. Each shimmering candle gives light by yielding its wax to the flame—a total sacrifice, given to illuminate—much as Christ did when he brought Christmas to earth long ago.

For a few short hours on one special night, these candle luminarias shine, but Dataw Island has many living luminarias—people aflame all year long, bringing light and warmth to our island and to the community around us. We see evidence of their sparkle on Dataw—in maintaining the butterfly garden, in serving Christmas lunch to island workers, in contributing to a special Christmas gift fund for island employees, in working on special projects, and in serving on many committees.

Their light is shed abroad to the community by Dataw residents who serve others by picking up highway trash to delivering meals to volunteering at schools, clubs and institutions; to giving both time and resources to numberous charities and service clubs to building houses for the needy. The luminosity list is expansive and far reaching to over thirty different organizations and hundreds of individuals in our community area.

"Light Up the Night" is a special way to celebrate the season for one evening, but Dataw's living luminarias keep the spirit of the season alive by lighting up the world all year long. In any community, there are those who give their time, talent, and treasure to illuminate the lives of others.

You are the light of the world. A city set on a hill cannot be hidden; nor does anyone light a lamp and put it under a basket

– Matthew 5:14-15

Christmas Green Giving

The Christmas gift-giving season is a wonderful opportunity for gardeners. For those who are always thinking *green*, giving green is a natural way of gifting almost anyone with something that will continue to bring joy long after the season has passed. I'm not talking about tucking a few dollar bills into a greeting card and being done with it. I'm talking about giving "greens" that are living, ones that perpetuate life and the natural beauty of our world. They can be in the form of seeds or seedlings that will replenish themselves to become a continual gift.

A green gift is suitable for almost anyone on any list: for Uncle Harvey who has enough greens in his wallet to buy whatever he wants, or for Grandson Charlie whose room is already filled to capacity with high-tech toys, or for Grandma Bessie who still hasn't worn the jewelry you gave her last year.

Consider the possibilities:

- Have a tree planted wherever the recipients choose, whether in their back yard or in California where millions have been destroyed
- Purchase seed packets to be sent to countries suffering from famine (one $2.60 packet can provide 200 lbs. of food)
- Give a subscription to a Plant or Rose of the Month Club for those who can care for them
- Donate in the name of the recipient to any organization or program that conserves nature or fosters gardening

These are but a few of the many gift possibilities that will not be quickly consumed and forgotten. As Shakespeare noted, "One touch of nature makes the whole world kin." By giving green, we enhance our shared environment and plant a promise that will continue for posterity, fulfilling the purpose of God's gift of plants and trees when He created them.

And God said, "Behold, I have given you every plant yielding seed that is on the face of all the earth, and every tree with seed in its fruit. You shall have them for food"

– Genesis 1:29

God's Garden of Gifts

Come now, December, and what do we see?
All kinds of gifts spread under a tree.
Oh, not the kind that at stores do abound,
But those we've been blessed with all the year round.

You won't find a bottle of costly perfume,
But a bouquet of fragrance to fill up a room -
With velvety petals and colors so bold
Their brilliance and beauty your eyes can behold.

No famous paintings for purchase to pay,
But radiant sunsets are ours every day.
Each one made special with brush strokes of love,
Wrapped with cloud-ribbons and tied from above.

No jewel-boxed diamonds, so costly and bright,
We're star-struck with billions that light up each night.
And the music we have you won't find on CDs,
Bird, wind, and rain sing unique melodies.

No need to go shopping online or at store
God's garden of gifts is outside the back door.
No need to set out and head for the mall
Look out the window for "one size fits all."

No credit card limits; these gifts are all free -
An abundance of treasures is under *each* tree.
Nothing man-made can compare in like measure
With what God has made for our joy and our pleasure.

*For His invisible attributes, namely, His eternal power and divine nature, have been
clearly perceived, ever since the creation of the world, in the things that have been made*

– Romans 1:20

New Year Resolutions

The New Year is at the gate, the clock is ticking loud and clear
I'll need to hurry if I'm to keep the resolutions I made last year!

Ever wonder where the whole idea of New Year's resolutions came from? It seems we can attribute to the Babylonians the idea of assessing the past and resolving to improve in the New Year. It caught on, obviously, and has continued to this day.

Of course, there's nothing wrong with wanting to improve oneself; I've tried it many times. In fact, the top three resolutions in America fit well into my list for the New Year, as they have for several new years in the past: to spend more time with family and friends, to lose weight, and to get fit. I've observed, however, that most of the time spent with family and friends is centered on *food*. Thus, the most exercise I get is the walk to the table and the elbow bend to the mouth. This seems a little counterproductive. While striving to fulfill the first resolution, I'm jeopardizing the other two!

Some slackers might say, "You can't break what you don't make." But for those who regard this wonderful garden in which we live, turning over a new leaf couldn't hurt. Producing new leaves does take time, and in a culture that has grown to expect instant gratification, resolutions requiring patience and commitment are challenging to keep.

Perhaps the wisest approach to making any changes is to consider resolutions we might keep for the New Day or even the New Hour rather than taking on a whole year to achieve. Success comes in small steps. As the New Year approaches, I hope all of us will consider carefully what we determine, so that our resolutions will not go in one year and out the other.

Forever is composed of nows

– Emily Dickinson

Swing from the Old—Grab Hold of the New

Watching my granddaughter traverse from swinging post to swinging post on a playground play pod, I noticed she had to let go of the pole she was holding to step to the next pod, even though both pods were swaying. Each move was executed with a mixture of reflection, consideration, trepidation, and anticipation, yet there was no retreat.

There is a lesson here for us to consider in the waning days of December and the approaching New Year. To gain a foothold on the next step, we have to release the one we're on. Of course, we're never assured that the next pod will be as comfortable, peaceful, or stable as we perceive the one we are about to leave behind. However, the swinging post we're clinging to may be so rocky that moving on just has to be better.

The reality is that life will go on, whether we choose to go with it or not. Even flowers must yield their blossoms to make new seeds, having been programmed to do so. Robert Beattie's poem "A Way to a Happy New Year" says it well:

To leave the old with a burst of song,
To recall the right and forgive the wrong,
To forget the thing that binds you fast
To the vain regrets of the year that's past

Add to that the wisdom of a grandchild who reached the other side of the pod and observed, "See, Grammy, it's not easy, but if you let go of the old one and grab hold of the new one, you can make it." I agree. Not only can we make it, but we can also go with grace.

Who forces time is pushed back by time; who yields to time finds time on his side

– The Talmud

A Gardener's New Year Resolution

To plow up new ground, turning over
Encrusted intentions to reveal fresh resolve
And new possibilities

To plant seeds of positive promise
Appreciating each one's unique potential
To grow and flourish

To tend to whatever each day brings
Accepting what sprouts – or doesn't -
Trusting in the Master plan

To pluck out "if only" or "what if" weeds
Before they subdue and choke out
The present unfolding reality

To gather in the matchless treasures
Etched in leaf, tree, and flower -
Hope upon everlasting hope

To take joy in the process, the labor
As well as the fruit of it all -
Life – the garden of blessings

So neither he who plants nor he who waters is anything, but only God who gives the growth. He who plants and he who waters are one and each will receive his wages according to his labor

– 1 Corinthians 3:7-8

January Gardeners

Most gardeners are optimists—even in January. The month was named for the mythical two-faced god Janus, who looked both forward and backward. However, gardeners to express *carpe diem*—they seize the day and look to the future. Many are either scanning garden catalogs for possibilities or plotting flower beds in their minds until temperatures allow them to work outdoors. Some may be actually starting seeds in egg cartons or nurturing seedlings in window boxes.

Charlie Brown was probably not a gardener. He kept thinking about what might have been. When Linus reminded him to look to today, he disagreed. "No, that's giving up. I'm still hoping yesterday will get better."

Our past gardens may be overgrown with evidence of successes and failures, just as our lives are. We can benefit by reflecting on both, but if we spend too much time cultivating thoughts of *if only* or *what if*, we'll miss the chance to plant today's crop. The best we can do about yesterday is to learn from it and make a better garden. To keep digging up the past is unproductive, unless we are plowing under the soil of disappointments and turning it over to reveal the fresh, fertile nutrients of hope that come from the depths of faith, grounded in what God assures will come.

So here's to all you January gardeners looking to dig in the "land of beginning again"—may your garden plans of today be filled with promising seeds that produce green shoots tomorrow in the soil of life. I can't wait to see what's "growing" to happen next.

. . . I do not consider that I have made it my own. But one thing I do: forgetting what lies behind and straining forward to what lies ahead

– Philippians 3:13

Planting Ahead

The story is told of a man who instructed his gardener to plant a certain type of tree. The gardener objected by saying the tree was slow growing and would take decades to mature. "Then," the man said, "We must plant it this morning, as we have no time to lose!"

As we begin a new year, many of us might pause to think about how we are redeeming our time. We reflect on the past and make resolutions and plans, keenly aware of that equalizing commodity of lifetime. Each of us has the same amount of time credited to our account each day, no one being richer or poorer where time is concerned. Unlike money, which can be borrowed or saved, time is redeemed at once and for once.

It's much like being given 1,440 dollars to spend each day with the admonition that what isn't spent is lost. For someone who loves to shop, this would not be a problem. The truth is, we *are* given 1,440 minutes to spend each day, and how we expend that time reveals the substance of our lives. We can neither borrow time from the promise of tomorrow nor recycle it from the waste of yesterday. It is a gift, the precious present, which we all receive in the same measure.

If we are like the man in the tree story, we will be wise in planting our time so that none will be lost, and our tree of life will grow.

So teach us to number our days that we may get a heart of wisdom

– Psalm 90:12

Some Interesting Dirt

January's Low Country garden, except for bright camellias and pansies, seems drab and lifeless. Deciduous trees openly bare their nakedness, summer annuals have long said farewell, ground covers are straggly, and even the sun has headed further south for the winter. It would appear that most plant life is taking a long winter's nap.

Not so! Beneath the very soil on which we tread there is a whole ecosystem at work in a complex living environment. Here we find some interesting dirt—each time we step on the ground, we are stepping on millions of microbes. These organisms have distinct functions: some are fertilizing the soil while others are breaking down dead matter, releasing nutrients into the earth.

Whether or not we see them working, they remain vital to our ecological system's health. The same might be said of how we regard some people. Based on observation alone, we catalog each other in unflattering ways, passing judgment on what is seen and assuming those perceptions to be true. If our hearts could be seen, like the soil, a different view might be the case. God may be working behind the "seens" to change them or us, so that the world around us will be nourished, and the result will be beautiful garden "scenes."

Just as we are taught not to judge people by appearances, we shouldn't judge the ground by its cover.

Do not judge by appearances, but judge with right judgment

– John 7:24

Everyday Valentines

February cannot pass
Without some thoughts in rhyme;
That saintly day is on its way -
The annual "red heart" time.

Some choose sending flowery cards
Others just send flowers;
Chocolates are also good
For sweetening up the hours.

The trouble with these gifts of love
Is that they're quickly gone -
Except, perhaps, the extra pounds
Those calories put on.

I like to think true valentines
Are daily acts of grace -
Kind words spoken, selfless deeds
That time cannot efface.

They do not fade or wither, yet
Are beautiful to see
Sincerest offerings – not compelled,
But given willingly.

They're treasures tucked inside the heart,
Memories living on -
A legacy of valentines
Cherished all year long!

Little children, let us not love in word or talk but in deed and in truth

– 1 John 3:18

Perspective

Looking at a plant that appeared shriveled and dying, I was ready to yank it up. Then, when I looked at the other side, I noticed some green leaves beginning to form. A different perspective stayed my hand. That can be true about our perspectives of our circumstances every day—just when we draw a conclusion about something, if we stop a moment and consider a broader view, we may see it differently.

We complain about too much rain while wildfires consume acres of property in the west. We dislike opening the mail to find bills to pay, but the homeless don't have such bills. We are finicky about the food we're served yet over 30% of what we produce in America ends up in the garbage and the number of undernourished people in India is equal to our U.S. population. Rain, bills and throw-away food might be welcomed by others; it's all a matter of perspective.

When we take a closer look at any of our circumstances and consider a wider standpoint, we might find more for which to be grateful than for being discontented. We need to stop and think— there are people who would love to have what we consider to be our "bad" situations.

Do all things without grumbling or questioning. . .

– Philippians 2:14

Of Love, Vines and Valentines

Ever notice how the vines on a mandavilla or clematis plant intertwine so tightly that we can't distinguish one from another? It occurs to me how this parallels the word *lovingkindness*, which appears many times in the book of Psalms. The compounding of these two benevolent actions make them truly inseparable; one can't be sincerely kind without loving nor truly loving without being kind. The essence of the one is inexorably intertwined with that of the other.

Each year we celebrate St. Valentine's Day with its various expressions of love and kindness. While the tradition of sending love messages is a good one, I like what another saint by the name of Augustine said about the subject: "What does love look like? It has hands to help others. It has feet to hasten to the poor and needy. It has eyes to see misery and want. It has ears to hear the sighs and sorrows of fellow men. That is what love looks like."

In Augustine's view, love is manifested through our deepest sensitivity to others' needs, followed by putting that love into sacrificial action. This is lovingkindness. We can see it in those who aid the victims in natural disasters: wildfires, mudslides, and devastating hurricanes.

We don't have to go far to find it in our own backyard. Neighbors and friends reach out to those suffering from a disabling disease, the loss of a loved one, or other kinds of heartbreak—those personal tsunamis and mudslides that overwhelm us. "Each man's grief is my own," a line from the 50s song, "No Man Is An Island," by way of John Donne's reflection, captures the whole idea of how our lives are intertwined.

God spread His lovingkindness abroad as an example of what our relationship should be with Him and with others. We need Him. We need each other. We need lovingkindness. Perhaps that's why the Master Gardener planted the idea in the first place.

For His lovingkindness is great toward us, and the truth of the LORD is everlasting.
Praise the LORD!

– Psalm 117:2 (NASB)

Every Heart – A Garden

The heart is like a garden
Where many things can grow
The crop that it produces there
Depends on what we sow

Thoughts begin the process
They are just like seeds
Some will bring forth harvests rich
While others only weeds

Whatever thoughts we nourish
If bitter, harsh or cold
They root and sprout within the heart
And multiply tenfold

If we would sow but kindness,
Mercy, grace, and love
The heart would be a garden
Like the Gardener's one above

Lush and full of blessings
Eternally pristine
Overflowing, reproducing
Only gardens green

So daily plant your garden
Take care to think your part
For what you sow you'll also reap
In the garden of your heart

Your heart is full of fertile seeds waiting to sprout
– Morihei Ueshiba

Say It with Flowers

Valentine's Day usually means giving or getting either a bouquet of fresh flowers or a box of chocolates. I used to prefer receiving chocolates, but as I have grown in several ways, including older, I now prefer flowers. I've learned that chocolates usually go to waist. And while some say fresh flowers

are a waste—*they don't last; they just wilt and die*—I believe for that brief, beautiful moment when roses stand tall in the vase or lilies open to saucer-size blossoms, they provide glorious beauty and refreshment to our senses.

Fresh flowers are God's spirit lifters, stress soothers, and day brighteners. Many of life's passages from birth to death are marked by giving and receiving flowers; memories of them are like scattered petals on life's pathways, yielding a calm, lingering fragrance to an otherwise hectic world. They cause us to consider how such intricate detail and unique colors could possibly be an accident of nature.

"A flower's appeal is in its contradictions—so delicate in form yet strong in fragrance, so small in size yet big in beauty, so short in life yet long on effect." – Terri Guillemets, *The Quote Garden*.

If you are trying to decide whether to send chocolates or flowers to your Valentine, I say forget the box of Godiva or Russell Stover, send a bouquet. Better yet, send a flowering plant that can be put in the garden as an ongoing gift to enjoy. The bonus is this: the remembrance of your choice will remain in the recipient's heart, not on her hips.

Flowers are the sweetest things God ever made, and forgot to put a soul into

– Henry Beecher

A Heart of True Love

True love is   a heart gift,
a willful offering   bestowed without
any expectation of   recompense or return.
The ultimate good of its object is its deepest desire -
selfless, sacrificial, it is an overflow of the Divine gift
of life itself – it is like air, sunshine, flowers, and rain,
shed abroad on all God's creation with manifold grace.
Unbridled, true love is bestowed – freely, undeserved,
unearned – given openly in word and deed, without
calling attention to itself. Like a flower gathered
from God's garden of grace, love blesses the one
who gives and the one to whom it is given –
springing forth, full of Faith and Hope.
Abiding forever, these three gifts of
Faith, Hope and Love reside deep
within the heart of all mankind.
Yet – while Faith and Hope
excel, one shines forth as
the greatest of all, yes!
It is the everlasting,
most marvelous
gift of all –
genuine
Love

. . . the greatest of these is love

– 1 Corinthians 13:13

Don't Judge the Ground by its Cover

Brown ground cover, bare branches, and shriveled vines—all we see on the winter landscape appears lifeless. It's said that seeing is believing, but we, like most gardeners, believe without seeing. Each time we plant a seed or bulb in the ground we are trusting what we *don't* see happening to cause it to become productive. This kind of blind trust could be called a "farmer's faith." We plant, water, and fertilize, and then wait expectantly for an unseen process to enrich and grow what we have entrusted to the soil.

What we might see if we could look into the dark underground of winter would be a fascinating picture of the synthesis of plant life. If we could see a cross-section, we would see hair-like tentacles reaching toward water, almost like multiple thirsty tongues stretching to get a drink.

And if we could watch a planted tulip bulb, we would witness it sprouting long tendrils—roots stretching deep into the ground so it can establish itself to feed on nutrients the soil is constantly providing. We would see how it assimilates such necessary nourishment, causing it to burst forth into our visible garden in its blossomed beauty.

So much is happening underground behind the "seens." We believe and trust that the amazing invisible process occurring will produce amazing "scenic" results. The fact of marvelous things occurring beyond our sight proves we should never judge the ground by its cover.

Now faith is the assurance of things hoped for, the conviction of things not seen

– Hebrews 11:1

Spring Again

The seasons have come full circle. The ever-moving, changing cycle repeats itself in the Master plan for life in this space and time. We marvel at how gardens demonstrate this sequence of birth, sprouting, maturity, rest, and rebirth and how the pattern parallels our lives. We, as the designated gardeners appointed to tend the gardens, can see a greater responsibility and reward beyond that of cultivating the earth. We are also called to tend to one another. That is our purpose, our legacy, the seeds for our posterity's gardens.

Our Endless Possibilities

Behold the little acorn
Lone and brown and small
Can we fathom it a mighty oak
Gigantic, broad, and tall?

In a mustard seed so tiny
How can we really see
By watered faith and proper care
It will become a tree?

If seeds have such potential
Within so small a core
Could we grow into something
We've never been before?

Could there be seeds of promise
In the soil of you and me
To learn to plant a garden full
Of possibility?

They will be called
oaks of righteousness,
a planting of the Lord
for the display of His splendor

— Isaiah 61:3

Can we commit to nurture
With minds and hands to bless
A community of brotherhood
Potentially endless?

Yes! If we dig in together
Devoted to this deed
We'll grow a godly garden here
From every grace-filled seed

And like the sturdy, standing oak
Or faithful mustard tree
Together what we sow today
Will be our legacy.

An Eternal Garden

God, who created the first garden, who set humanity above all creatures and put His spirit within, who placed eternity in the heart of people, will bring those who trust in his Son, Jesus Christ, to a place of peace and rest. He will fulfill the promise made by His Son's sacrifice that they will live again, just as Jesus does. Just as winter is only a passing season on earth, so is our life in earth's garden. Life has no end for believers in Christ because an eternal garden awaits them—a heavenly garden where the Tree of Life grows and flourishes forever.

So while the earth remains, we look with hope to the passing of each season, living, learning, and trusting the Master Gardener to cultivate our faith as year upon year we exist for a time in this wonderful garden where we are planted.

So we do not lose heart. Though our outer self is wasting away, our inner self is being renewed day by day. For this light momentary affliction is preparing for us an eternal weight of glory beyond all comparison, as we look not to the things that are seen but to the things that are unseen. For the things that are seen are transient, but the things that are unseen are eternal

– 2 Corinthians 4:16-18

End Notes

Nothing to Sneeze At – Haltiwanger, John, Ed. "People Who Appreciate Nature Are Happier, Healthier And More Innovative." Elite Daily, 06 May 2015.

Musings of a South Carolina Transplant – Jackson, Marcus. "Transplanting Trees and Shrubs." North Dakota State University Extension Service Circular F.

Happiness In Bloom – Rutgers, the State University of New Jersey. "The Evolutionary Triumph Of Flower Power." ScienceDaily. ScienceDaily, 25 May 2005. www.sciencedaily.com

Gathering and Scattering – "The Legend of the 5 Kernels of Corn." www.teacherweb.com.

Steps to Peace – "What Are Healing Gardens? Taking Charge of Your Health & Wellbeing." University of Minnesota, July 10, 2013.

The Arbor Day Legacy – "Celebrate Arbor Day Guidebook." www.arborday.org. National Arbor Day Foundation.

Photo and Illustration Acknowledgements

Spring, Fall and **Winter** page photos taken by the author on Dataw Island, South Carolina.

Summer page photo courtesy of Susan Blackburn, Dataw Island, South Carolina.

How to Spell Dataw Spring watercolor, courtesy of Susan Blackburn.

Grace watercolor, courtesy of Susan Blackburn.

Seeds and Stitches quilt garden photo courtesy of www.quiltgardens.com and the Heritage Trail, Elkhart, Indiana. Used by permission.

Various color photos throughout the book were free downloads from www.morguefile.com. Used by permission.

Photos and illustrations not specifically credited were obtained from public accessible sources online presented as free and/or non-copyrighted photos or illustrations.

Special Acknowledgements

The book you hold in your hands would be less than I envisioned had not certain people contributed to its production. My friend, Susan Blackburn, shared her artistic talent by allowing me to use her photographs and watercolors of which some were especially created for the book. Jan Ackerson provided her expertise by editing the manuscript and helping me craft it into a better offering. Rachel Greene used her skills to layout the work in an attractive readable format and her husband, Joel, captured the theme of the book by designing the beautiful cover.

I am indebted to all of these individuals for their contributions. Most of all, I am grateful for Jesus Christ, without whom nothing I do would be of any great value at all.

About the Author

Sandra Fischer was a former teacher and Christian bookstore owner in Indiana before retiring in 2001 and moving to Dataw Island, South Carolina. In addition to writing inspirations for the local garden club, several of her stories have appeared in various anthologies, including: *Faithwriters—Hidden in the Hymns, Grandmother, Mother and Me, Wisdom of our Mothers,* and *Friends of Inspire Faith.* She is a regular contributor to Faithwriters.com. To learn more about her or to read more of her works, visit these links:

http://www.faithwriters.com/member-profile.php?id=1729
http://fisch-lines.blogspot.com/
http://www.amazon.com/Sandra-Fischer/e/B00ISC2GA4/

CPSIA information can be obtained
at www.ICGtesting.com
Printed in the USA
LVOW05s1222221115

463629LV00002B/2/P